TOHORÃ

The Story of Fyffe House, Kai Kõura

TOHORĀ

The Story of Fyffe House, Kai Kōura

JAN HARRIS

NEW ZEALAND HISTORIC PLACES TRUST
POUHERE TAONGA

ACKNOWLEDGEMENTS
The New Zealand Historic Places Trust/Pouhere Taonga acknowledges with gratitude the assistance of the New Zealand Lottery Grants Board, the family of the late Margaret Wood of Kai Kōura, the Kai Kōura Historical Society and the Canterbury Museum.

Author's Acknowledgements
I should like to thank the many people and organisations who have assisted with information and illustrations, and who have worked on the house and display: Cindy Beavis, Stephen Cashmore, Alan Cragg, Chris Cochran, John Daniels, Department of Survey and Land Information, Jim Espie, the late Mary Forbes, Jack Fry, Pam Garbes, Gwen Gray, Charles Low, Beverley McCulloch, Neil McKay, Bob and Andrew McTavish, Kathleen Major, Māori Language Commission, National Library, Terence O'Donnell, Charles Scott, Michael Trotter, Nick Tupara and Dean Whiting. All illustrations are acknowledged in the text.

I owe a special debt of thanks to Te Aue Davis, who has corrected the Māori words and place names in the text. This sets a new standard for the Trust, and is particularly appropriate for the first book published by the Trust since the introduction of its new Act.

First published 1994
by New Zealand Historic Places Trust
PO Box 2629 Wellington
New Zealand

ISBN 0 908577 21 4

Design and production by Stephen Barnett/Bookmakers, Auckland
Typesetting by Ward Four Design, Auckland
Printed in Singapore by South Wind Production

Title page drawing by John Creagh

Contents

FYFFE HOUSE
is owned and maintained for the people of New Zealand
by the New Zealand Historic Places Trust
Pouhere Taonga

ONE

The Earliest People

FYFFE HOUSE is in Kai Kōura, Marlborough. From its verandah one can see across the bay to the Seaward Kai Kōura Range, snow-capped for most of the year; rising ground behind shelters the house from cold southerly winds. The house was there before the town, being part of the first European settlement in the area. This settlement, established to hunt tohorā, the southern right whale, was the Wai ō Puka whaling station, around the point at what is now Armers Beach.

Long before this, however, another people had found the Kai Kōura Peninsula a favourable site for food gathering. The very name, Kai Kōura, is associated with food, meaning 'to eat a crayfish', and is a contraction of the full name, Kā Ahi Kai Kōura a Tama Ki Te Rangi, 'the fire on which Tama Ki Te Rangi cooked his crayfish'.[1]

Human activity has taken place in this region for nearly a thousand years. Archaeological investigation, from 1973 onwards, established that it was occupied by Archaic Māori (sometimes called moa hunters) more than 900 years ago. Bones found included not only moa, but also seal, fish and shellfish, and the extinct rail, swan and goose. The people who lived there used flint knives and bone fish-hooks, had shell and bone ornaments, and used moa eggs as water containers.[2]

The moa egg found by George Fyffe in 1857. *(Museum of New Zealand/Te Papa Tongarewa)*

Europeans first found evidence of these early people and their connection with the now extinct moa when it was reported in 1857 that:

> Mr Fyfe had found a Moa's egg, at the Kai Kora's, while digging the foundation for his store. It is a foot long, about 6 inches in diamater *(sic)*, and 27 inches in circumference. The shell is the 16th part of an inch in thickness. A hole is drilled in the end of it, and the egg must have been considered of great value to the natives, as it was found deposited at the head of a skeleton, with a number of very large poenamu *(sic)* axes. Mr Fyfe, we understand, is going to send them home to the British Museum.[3]

George Fyffe also placed considerable value on the egg. He sent it

This unique harpoon head made of moa bone was recovered during an archaeological excavation at the Fyffe site. It resembles those from sites of a similar age in the Marquesas Islands group. *(Canterbury Museum, courtesy Beverley McCulloch)*

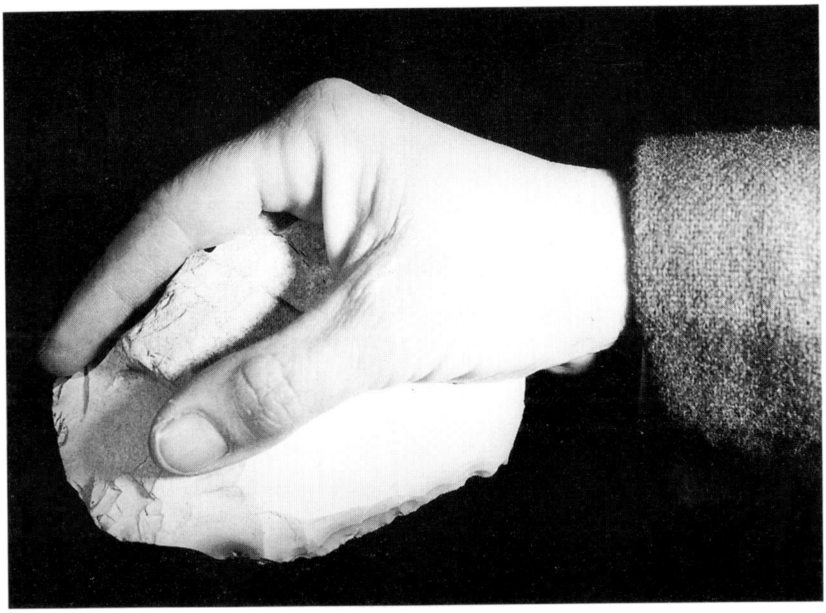

This large stone knife is made of local 'flint' found in the Āmuri limestone and was also recovered during an archaeological excavation at the Fyffe site. It was probably used for butchering larger game such as moa or seals. *(Canterbury Museum, courtesy Beverley McCulloch)*

to Wellington and asked for 'a brass plate fixed on the top of the case with "George Fyffe Kaikoura" engraved thereon'.[4] It was sent to the New Zealand Exhibition of 1865 in Dunedin, and was later sent to England.[5] The largest moa egg ever found, it is now in the Museum of New Zealand/Te Papa Tongarewa, Wellington.

Later Māori activity in the area included fowling and fishing. It is possible that there were also stone-walled kūmara gardens near Fyffe House 300-400 years ago, although the evidence for this is disputed.[6]

The area is thought to have been occupied from the mid fifteenth

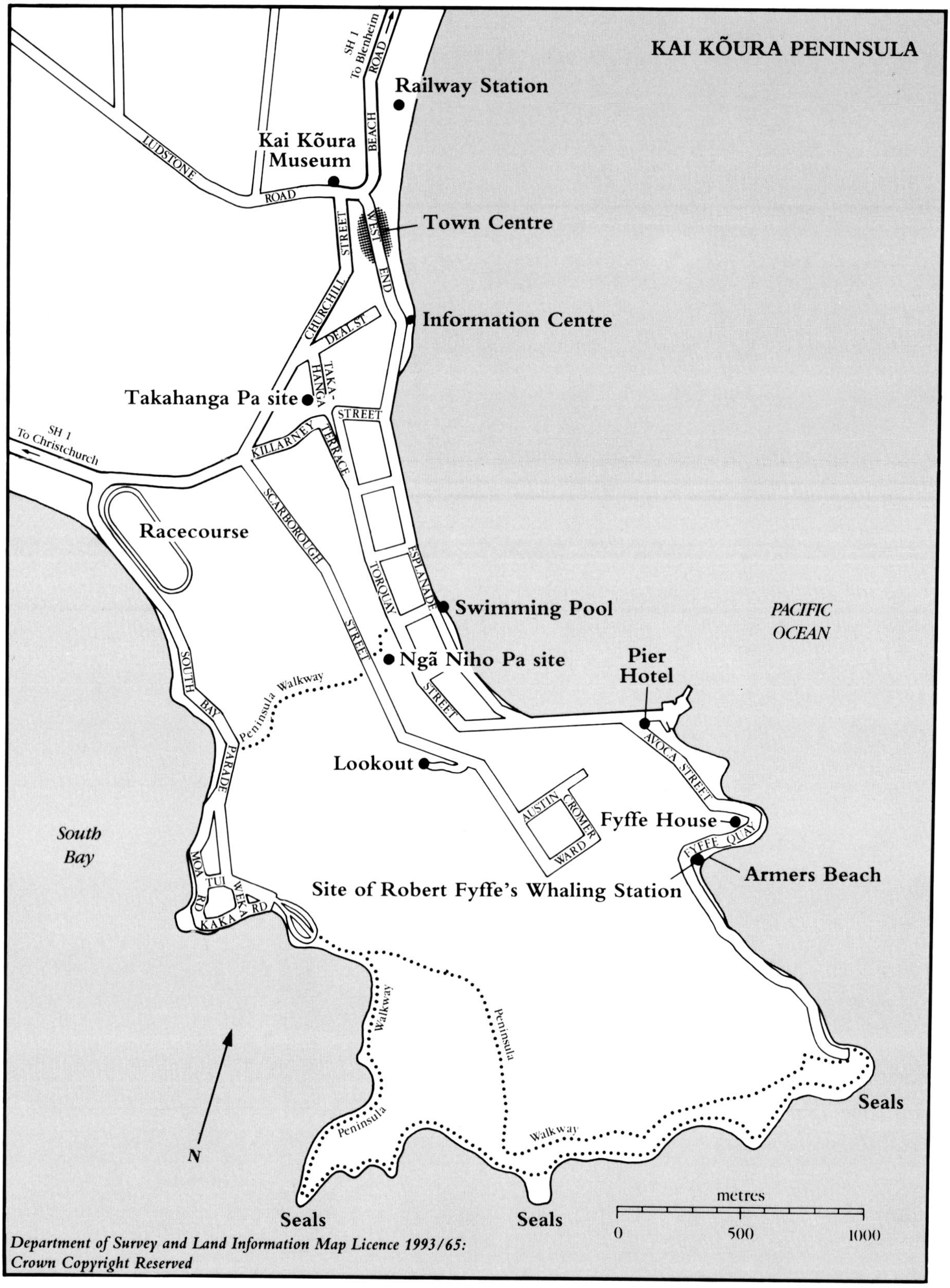

Map of Kai Kōura Peninsula. *(Drawn by Tim Galloway)*

to the mid sixteenth centuries by the Māori people known as Waitaha. They were followed by Kāti Mamoe and then by Kāi Tahu who migrated from the North Island in the seventeenth century and conquered and intermarried with Kāti Mamoe. Kai Kōura was settled by the Kāti Kuri sub-tribe of Kāi Tahu.[7]

There were several pā in the Kai Kōura area; Takahanga, dating from the early seventeenth century, was the dominant pā. For about 200 years it protected both the coastal trade route and the inland route over the Wai au plains the Māori used to obtain pounamu (nephrite or greenstone).[8]

Takahanga is still a place of great significance to the Kāi Tahu people and was gazetted an historic reserve in 1975. At the request of Kāi Tahu it was declared a traditional site by the New Zealand Historic Places Trust in 1984. A marae has been established there recently by Kāti Kuri; the whare tupuna (Maru Kai Tātea), gateway and garden are on the sites of the same features, as revealed by archaeological excavations in 1980 and 1982.[9] Whale watching, which since 1989 has attracted thousands of tourists to Kai Kōura, is a marae-based operation.

In the early nineteenth century Kāi Tahu were threatened by Ngāti Toa from the Kapiti area of the North Island, near Cook Strait. The Ngāti Toa were led by the well-known Te Rauparaha, who had brought them to Kapiti from their original home in Kawhia, 400 kilometres to the north. In a battle in 1830[10] many Kai Kōura Kāi Tahu were killed, or taken to Kapiti, not returning until the late 1830s.[11]

By the mid 1830s Te Rauparaha had conquered much of the northern half of the South Island. However, the Ngāti Toa failed to establish occupation rights, and had retreated by the late 1830s. The area is still occupied by Kāi Tahu.

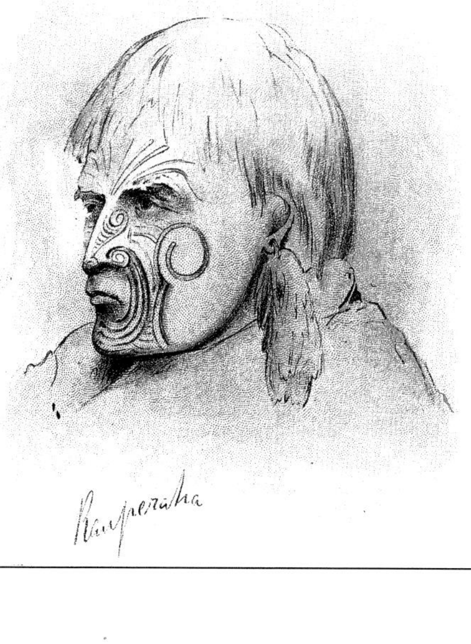

Te Rauparaha by J. Gilfillan. *(Alexander Turnbull Library)*

Kai Kōura Whakatau.
(Kai Kōura Museum)

When Te Rauparaha attacked, the Kāi Tahu leader in the Kai Kōura area was absent and thus survived to guide his people through a new experience — settlement by Europeans, which was facilitated by the smaller number of Kāi Tahu left. This leader was Kai Kōura Whakatau. Described as a large and handsome man, he, with his two wives, lived at the settlement of Mikonui near Āmuri Bluff, south of the Kai Kōura Peninsula. He decided where whalers could establish bases, and was the advocate for his people until 1868, when he died after falling from his horse.[12]

In 1847 the Wairau Purchase, including the Kai Kōura area, had been signed by the Ngāti Toa. The Kāi Tahu disputed their right to dispose of the part of this land north of Kaiapoi though at first with little success. During 1851-53 the Kai Kōura Māori obstructed some survey and building work; finally, in 1856, the government sent an official to Kaiapoi to investigate. His view was that the Kāi Tahu were entitled to compensation for the land north of Kaiapoi already sold by the Ngāti Toa. The Kaiapoi Purchase of 5 February 1857 was signed by Kai Kōura Whakatau and other leaders, who received £200 to divide amongst the claimants.[13]

In February 1859 the Assistant Native Secretary for the South Island, James Mackay, arrived at Kai Kōura where he was joined by Kai Kōura Whakatau and other leaders. Some Māori had complained that they had not received compensation from the Kaiapoi Purchase for their share in the land between the Huru nui and Wai au rivers. After negotiation, a deed of sale, the Kaikoura Purchase, was drawn up, and for £300 the Crown obtained over 400 million hectares, less Māori reserves of 8,957 hectares. By this time, however, Europeans were already squatting on the land, and had long since established whaling stations on the shore.[14]

TWO

The Old Whaling Days

WHALERS (and sealers) first came to New Zealand in 1792. Initially, whalers pursued sperm whales — deep sea whales — in boats launched from a parent ship, and the oil was processed on board. The whaling ships cruised in the Pacific in the winter, hunting near the New Zealand coast from October to May. New Zealand harbours, particularly in the Bay of Islands, were useful ports of call where the Māori could provide fresh food, water, timber and flax rope in return for muskets. The ships were British in the early years to about 1825, American from 1830-60, French from 1835-50 and Australasian from 1825-50.[1]

By 1841 fewer ships were visiting, partly because of the decline in whale numbers, partly because they could obtain supplies more cheaply elsewhere in the Pacific and perhaps mostly because New Zealand had become a British colony in 1840 with laws and customs duties.[2] This made whaling in New Zealand waters less profitable.

Well before this time, shore whaling had been established, hunting tohorā, the baleen or right whale (*Balaena glacialis,* formerly *B. australis,* called 'right' because it was easy to catch). The advantages were less danger, particularly from fire, as the trypots were set up on the beach, and more comfort, including fresh food and water. The oil processed on shore was superior in quality, because fresher, and got to its markets sooner. Perhaps the most important advantage was that less capital was needed to set up a shore station. The major saving was the cost of the whaling ship; a little brig or schooner cost far less, could serve several shore stations, and could transport people and supplies along the coast in the off-season.[3]

The shore-based whaling season was between May and October when the right whales travelled up the east coast of the South Island and through Cook Strait to Cloudy Bay and up the North Island coast to the South Taranaki Bight — the major breeding areas. From the 1830s — the peak decade of whaling — there was also 'bay whaling'.

This involved whaling ships that anchored in Cloudy Bay, Banks Peninsula, Otago and Bluff harbours, hunting the right whale. However, because the whales taken in bay and shore whaling were mostly cows and calves the supply was soon depleted; by 1845 tohorā, the right whales, were almost exterminated. In spite of protection for most of the twentieth century they are still rare, though numbers are increasing.

The first New Zealand shore-based whaling stations were established in the late 1820s. From 1829 through to the 1840s many stations were founded on the south and east coasts of the North and South Islands. It is probable that there were over 80, though some sources put the total as high as 113; however, it is unlikely that more than 50 ever operated at any one time.[4] The New Zealand stations were Australian-owned at first, but as whales became scarce little co-operatives based on Wellington capital were usual.[5] They varied in size, but a station operating four boats — the same number of boats as a whaling ship — needed at least 30 men. Most of the men, apart from craftsmen such as

'Going on right whale'. *(Making New Zealand Collection, Alexander Turnbull Library)*

Position of crew in a whale boat.
(Alexander Turnbull Library)

Cutting the blubber of a whale.
(Alexander Turnbull Library)

coopers, received a share of the profits, known as the lay; the proportion varied according to rank, the headsman of each boat receiving the highest share. From this, or the prospect of it, the men obtained credit from the owner for food, clothing, tobacco and liquor.

While shore life might pose fewer risks than life on board a whaling ship, once out at sea in the open long boats, the risks were similar, and New Zealand coastal waters claimed many lives. When the lookout sighted a whale the longboats were launched. The harpooner, when the boat was close enough to the whale, would throw the harpoon, attached to a hemp line coiled in a tub. A second harpoon was kept in each boat in case the first missed or the whale broke free. When the whale had tired sufficiently it was killed with a lance and the tail tendons cut with a razor-sharp whaling spade. This was done to try to prevent the boat being smashed by the large and powerful flukes. The boat crew towed the whale ashore and processing began.[6]

The blubber was cut up and melted in the large trypots to extract the oil, which was skimmed off and poured into wooden barrels for shipment. The barrels or casks also served to store or transport water, liquor, food, clothing and other goods. They were assembled, often from precut staves, by the cooper, a skilled and essential worker.

A whaler's hut at Kai Kõura. *(Alexander Turnbull Library)*

Coopers and carpenters on a ship were roughly equivalent to a naval petty officer in rank, and earned more money than the seamen. At shore stations local settlers also valued their skills.

Whale oil was used as a lubricant, but was more important as lamp fuel before kerosene was widely available (from the 1860s). The used blubber was burned as fuel at the station, though it made a great deal of smoke; the ashes were used for cleaning. Another valuable part of the right whale was the baleen, a horny substance inside the whale's mouth usually referred to commercially as whalebone. It was used extensively for umbrella and corset ribs. The flesh and bones were not used, though bone was sold in Polynesian and Melanesian islands as a form of ivory, or carved by whalers at sea to make decorative items known as scrimshaw work.[7] At Fyffe House the bones also served as foundations, and here and at some whaling stations they were used as fence posts.

Before 1840 Māori exercised some control over the stations; those in the Kapiti area, for instance, were under the protection of Te Rauparaha. Most whaling stations employed Māori men, and some women, as boat crew, and whalers usually had Māori wives; this was often insisted upon by Māori leaders.[8] European wives were rare. The women cooked and cleaned, gardened and looked after any stock, such as chickens, goats or cows. The gardens provided the staple potatoes, and other vegetables such as cabbage, turnips, corn or kūmara, depending on the locality. The basic food consisted of pork, potatoes, bread (a luxury not usually available at sea) and fish, with wild pigeons and sometimes fern root supplied by the whalers' Māori wives' relations. Whale meat, a delicacy to Māori, was not usually eaten by whalers.[9]

The average whaler's hut was adapted from Māori construction (and in turn influenced Māori huts, for instance in the provision of windows, chimneys and beds). It was built of wattle and daub, or sawn timber where this was available, with a roof thatched with reeds or rushes. Higher than a Māori hut, it also had a taller door, with hinges, windows — usually glassless — and a fireplace. Often simply one large room with an earth floor, it was furnished with bunks, a long table and benches, and perhaps whale vertebrae as stools for the many children. Clothing, tools and equipment hung on the walls or from the ceiling.[10] Apart from the bones, and the smoke and smell from the try-pots (which the occupants were quite accustomed to), it was not very different from the hut of early settlers, and this is indeed what many whalers became.

Whalers did not become wealthy. While prices for oil and whalebone were high in London, freight costs were also high, so it was usual to send the oil to Wellington, where, however, the merchants did not pay so well. Income was supplemented by trading activities and also by pastoral farming. This required land, which could be obtained through a whaler's wife's family rights, or by purchase from the Māori. After 1840 these purchases were examined by a Land Commissioner; small transactions were usually confirmed.[11]

Right whales were becoming scarce near New Zealand by the 1840s and there were no controls. Many whalers believed that competition from, for example, French or American whalers was the problem, refusing to admit the truth: that too many whales had been caught, and that the wrong whales — cows and calves — had been taken. Eventually, however, the number of right whales caught declined even further, until by 1850 there were virtually none. Whalers realised that there was no future in whaling. They had to decide to settle in New Zealand, farming or practising a trade such as coopering or carpentry; or leave to seek whales in other waters.

THREE

Robert Fyfe and the Wai ō Puka 'Fishery'

SHORE WHALING came to Kai Kōura after the peak years, but the man who initiated it there had been whaling in New Zealand waters during that boom time. Robert Fyfe[1] arrived in New Zealand in 1836 on the schooner *Industry,* with fellow passengers Jacky and Betty Guard and their children. Robert, baptised Alexander Robert in February 1811 at St Martin's, Perthshire, Scotland, had been a farm labourer and apprenticed to a wheelwright, but left at the age of 19 for a life at sea.[2]

On arrival in New Zealand he worked for a few years in the Marlborough whale industry with John Murray, with whom he established a shore based whaling station at Kai Kōura in 1842, the first in that area. This was the Wai ō puka station, or 'fishery', to the south of Fyffe House; it was located where the Wai ō Puka stream runs into the sea at what is now Armers Beach, formerly Fyffe Cove. The station was also known as Fyffe's or Fyfe's station or 'fishery'. A particular advantage of this site is that, in addition to the stream, there is a fresh water spring near the beach, uncovered at low tide.[3] The whalers squatted on the land, apparently with Māori permission, though it is probable that payments were made for its use.[4] The capital for the venture was supplied by John Wade, a Wellington merchant, and the oil and bone were handled by the Wellington firm of Waitt and Tyser.

In the autumn of 1843 Robert, with four whale boats, engaged 40 men for the winter season.[5] Their first priority must have been shelter: several huts for the men and a house for Robert, and a boat shed, try works and blubber stage were built. Beside the stream was a garden, which would have supplied potatoes. Around the point from the fishery (as it was called) was the cooper's house. The cooper, the essential maker of casks or barrels for whale oil, was 24-year-old Thomas Howell, from 'British America', who received £7 a month (the cook received £3 a month; the carpenter and the whalers, all seamen, received a share of the profits).[6]

The cooper's wing in 1977. *(Chris Cochran)*

It is the cooper's house, built before 1852,[7] which is believed to be the eastern wing of Fyffe House. This has two rooms, each with a French window opening onto a verandah. One room also has a single door to the verandah, and there is evidence (from lines on the floor boards) that this originally opened into an entrance hall with a store room behind.[8] This part of the house, known as the cooper's wing, is now the curator's quarters. It originally had a hipped roof covered with hand-split tōtara shingles, as revealed by examination in 1990.[9] A particularly interesting feature is the whale bone piles, which in New Zealand may be unique to Kai Kōura; they can be seen from the verandah, behind the seat.

The original hand-split shingles on the cooper's wing. *(Chris Cochran)*

A brief interruption to the work of the station occurred when the whalers heard of the Wairau incident. On 17 June 1843 Captain Arthur Wakefield and several other Europeans were killed while trying to arrest Te Rauparaha and another chief for resisting the survey of land which the Māori had denied having sold. The warlike attitude of Māori travelling south made the whalers feel unsafe and most went to Wellington. However, no further incidents were reported and they seem to have returned fairly soon. Despite this interruption, 130 tuns (casks) of oil were sent to Wellington between April and October 1843.[10]

The following year Murray established another Kai Kōura whaling station at South Bay. Murray seems to have taken little active part in either venture and by the end of the 1845 season Robert Fyfe was the sole owner of both stations.[11] By 1845 his Wellington financier and contractor was William Fitzherbert, who agreed to supply food, clothing and other necessary supplies, including cash to pay off the men. Supplies for the 1845 season included:

> 6 tons of Meat, Beef and Pork at 36/- per cwt
> 6 tons of Flour at 70/- per 100 lbs
> 1500 lbs of Sugar at 4½ d per lb
> 260 lbs of Ration Tea at 2/- per lb
> 4 cwt of soap at 48/- per cwt
> 5 New Zealand Whalelines at 75/- ea
> 1 keg Negrohead Tobacco, superior quality at 14d per lb
> 5 doz pairs Boots and Shoes, half of each, at 12/- per Pair
> 3 doz Pairs of Drawers at 60/- per dozen
> 12 Monkey Jackets at 12/- ea
> 3 doz Pairs of Worsted Stockings at 30/- per doz
> 24 pairs Moleskin Trousers at 12/- per Pair.[12]

To avoid dispute at the end of the season, a standard price of £10 or £12 a tun for oil and £40 a ton for bone was agreed at the time of signing on. At these rates, in 1845 a headsman would have earned almost £90; a pulling hand, however, would have received just under £20.[13] Most of this would have been spent on supplies, particularly if liquor was bought. Rum was said to be of equal importance to meat in station supplies, and whalers were notorious for drunkenness.[14]

Robert Fyfe's whaling success continued for a time, with 72 tuns of oil in 1844, 110 in 1845, 119 in 1846 — but only 35 in 1847.[15] Diversification began in that year with the purchase of the eight-ton schooner *Fidele,* which shipped supplies for both whalers and settlers in Marlborough and Canterbury. By 1849 Robert Fyfe, like many other whalers, had turned to farming, initially acquiring land by squatting. He grazed a flock of sheep for Wellington businessman Robert Waitt (with whom he had been involved earlier), sharing the annual wool clip and increase of the flock. In 1851, with competition from other settlers and Māori attitudes to land hardening, Robert applied for a depasturage[16] licence for his Kahu Tara Run, south of Kai Kōura, though the licence was only secured after his death.[17]

The land around the whaling station itself was unsuitable for sheep; Edmund Norman, who surveyed the area for the government in 1852, reported it as:

> entirely unfit for cultivation . . . in a swampy state — this circumstance added to very scanty feed would not tend to make it a desirable run for sheep. The soil throughout is poor, dry and sandy and covered with coarse grass, Toe toe, Tutu and Fern, nothing else growing except in the

> gullies where there is some Koromiko, Fucia and other shrubs of that kind, of little use even as firewood . . . The nearest Timber is about five miles from the [whaling] Station . . .[18]

Robert was the first pastoralist in the Kai Kōura region, and on his death in 1854 had amassed considerable property. In addition to the 'improvements' at the whaling station, valued at £310 (and including his house, valued at £30, and the cooper's, valued at £15),[19] he owned two seven-oared and two five-oared whale boats, a considerable quantity of whaling gear, household effects and stores, 21 casks of oil, 20 bales of wool, 1,778 sheep, 192 goats and a mule. The estate was eventually valued at over £6,000.[20]

Main illustration: Edmund Norman's survey of the whaling station area. Note the cooper's house. *(National Archives) Inset:* Edmund Norman's 1852 sketch of the whaling station. The house on the right is probably Robert Fyfe's own; the fenced area is the garden. *(National Archives)*

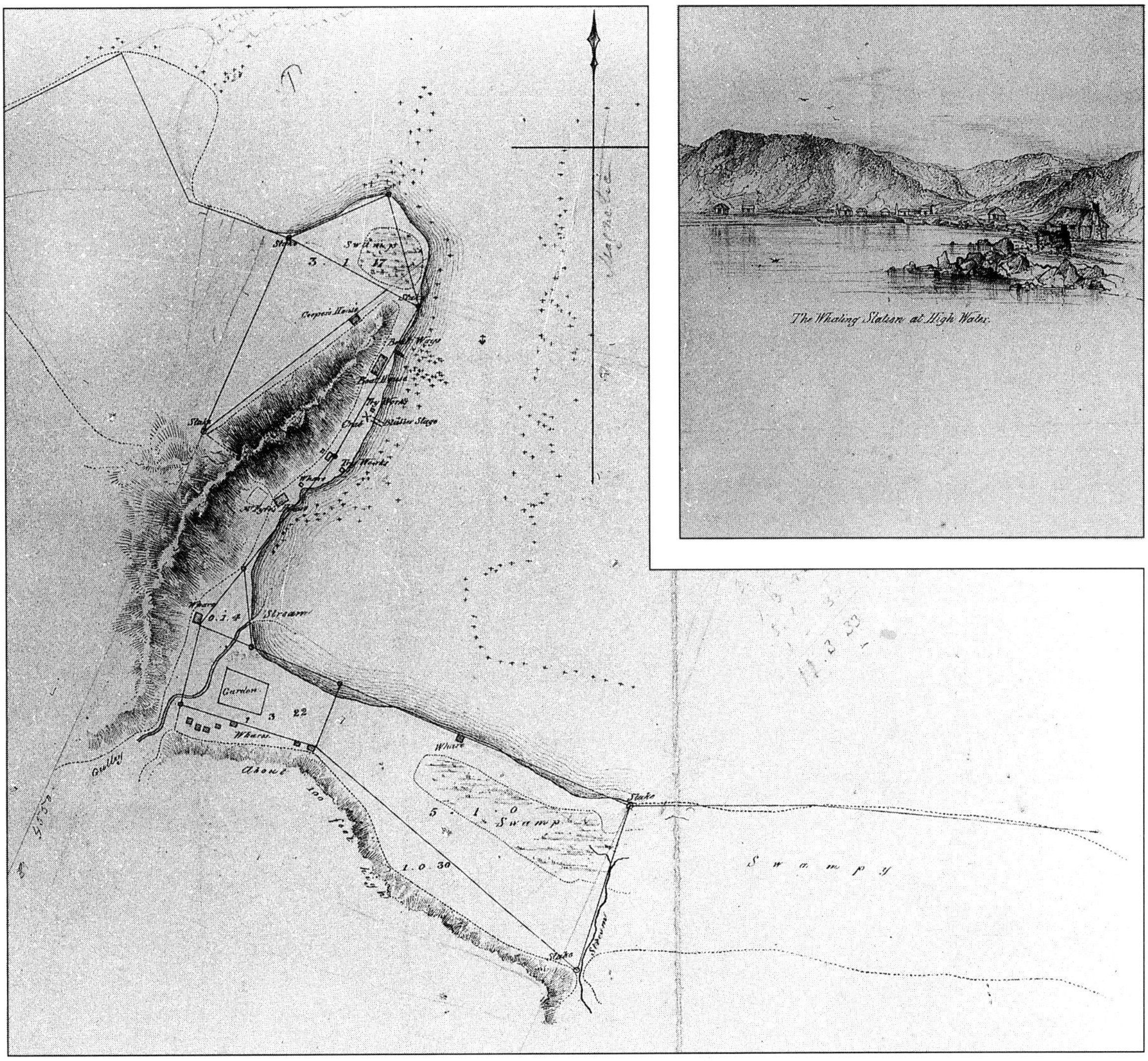

FOUR

George Fyffe, Settler

GEORGE FYFFE, a law student at Edinburgh University, was Robert's cousin and was invited to join him in New Zealand, arriving in Wellington in December 1853. However, in April 1854 Robert and his Māori crew member, Tani, were drowned when the *Fidele*, transporting whale oil to Wellington, was capsized and wrecked south of Cape Campbell. The bodies were buried on shore and the authorities in Wellington and George Fyffe were notified.[1] Robert's will, drawn up in 1852, left everything in trust for his next of kin. Advertisements were placed by Robert Hart, a solicitor in Wellington, seeking 'The Heir-at-law, and Next-of-kin of Robert Fyfe or Fyffe'.[2] Eventually — in 1862 — Robert's sister Elizabeth Laird arrived from New York to claim the estate, which was finally settled in 1864. The estate had been administered by the executors, Kenneth Bethune and George Hunter of Wellington. Elizabeth received most of the personal estate (valued at £6,224.17s.1d. — a large sum at that time) and effects, and her son, William Laird, and Wellington merchant John Johnstone were to act as trustees.[3]

George Fyffe had expected to obtain something from Robert's estate; he noted in his diary, 'My cousin's letter to me contains a promise of assistance in pecuniary matters . . . and had he made out a will after I went down with him I am certain it would have been in my favour. I also am of the opinion that none of his other relations will ever be able to make out a claim . . .'[4] However, he was to be disappointed, and the long wait to have matters settled may have contributed to his eventual lack of financial success. He may well have put less effort into his own ventures than he should have done, in the expectation that he would inherit Kahu Tara.

He had bought the whaling equipment and 'the right to whale' from the estate in 1854. However, whales were now rare, except for a good season in 1857. Sheep farming was George's major activity and he also obtained from the estate a three year lease on Robert's Kahu

Tara Run. He appears to have continued supervising this estate for several years and had a house there,[5] though resident managers were appointed.[6] Several men were employed, both at the whaling station and at Kahu Tara, including some whalers turned shearer. Some were American — 'Yankee Bill' (William Smith) for example.[7] George's employees also included a number of Māori, some of whom he had taught to shear.[8]

George Fyffe.
(Kai Kōura Museum)

His expenses must have been considerable. In 1857-58, for example, there were 17 men to whom he paid wages. These varied: Yankee Bill was paid 20/- a week for 'ordinary work' and 25/- a week while shearing, Kai Ruru was paid £35 a year as a shepherd, Edwin Cole got £40 a year as a cook, John Glennon £60 a year 'to drive bullocks and brake in four if required so to do', and Mr Richard Rothwell was engaged as 'working overseer' for £80 per annum.[9] George was still employing 18 men in 1863.[10] In addition to wages he had accounts for provisions, liquor and shipping — he seems to have chartered vessels for carrying stores and wool between Wellington and the east coast of the South Island.[11] George's sheep farming and trading seem to have yielded enough profit by the early 1860s for him to buy or lease a considerable amount of land, including the site on which Fyffe House stands.

Robert Fyfe had applied for a Crown Grant for this land — 80 acres (198 hectares), for which he paid £40 — but after his death the

The whaling station in 1863.
(From an original painting owned by the Macmillan family, Christchurch)

The land bought in 1862-64 by George Fyffe comprised rural sections 29-37, 40-48, and suburban sections 114, 145 and 224-225. Fyffe House is on section 224, the whaling station was on section 225.
(Mt Fyffe Survey District 1879, Alexander Turnbull Library)

application was cancelled and the money he paid was returned.[12] In 1861 George, who had apparently just discovered the cancellation, was anxious about his title to the 80 acres, and was considering petitioning the Governor 'to allow me . . . to purchase the ground whereon my Homestead stands without being put up to auction.'[13] The district was about to be surveyed and the town of Kai Kōura laid out by Joseph Ward. The first blocks of land were auctioned in 1862 and George bought several lots. Among them was a private sale of Suburban Sections 224 and 225, totalling 80 acres, for which he paid £40. Section 225, 75 acres (185 hectares), contained the whaling station;

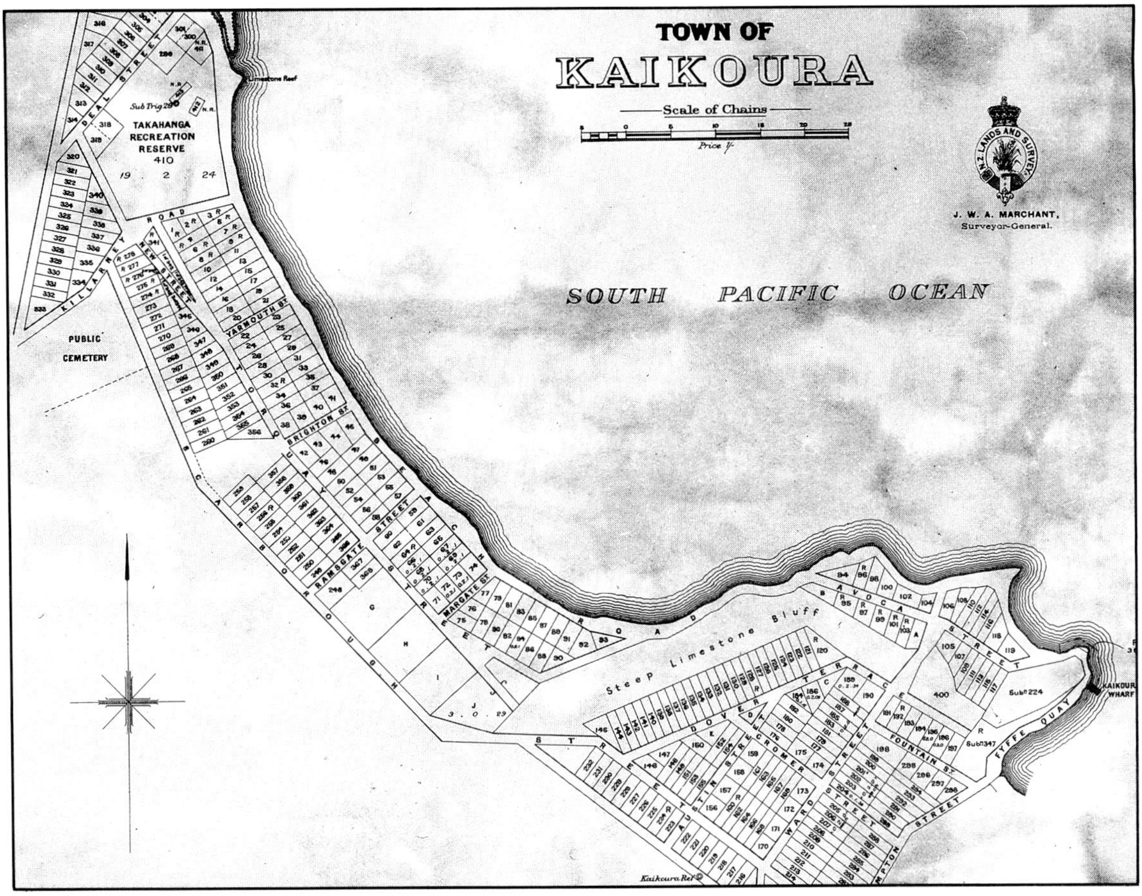

Kai Kõura Town sections owned by George Fyffe, mostly adjoining the Fyffe House site.
(Town of Kaikoura, 1902, Alexander Turnbull Library)

Section 224, on which Fyffe House stands, was just under 5 acres (12 hectares), and was marked 'Homestead' in the Sale Book.[14] George eventually obtained Crown Grants for this land on 4 July 1866.[15]

In 1864 George also bought several town sections along the seafront, adjoining Section 224.[16] In 1863 a jetty was built, on or near the site of the now redundant whaling station's 'boat way'.[17] The purchase of the town sections in addition to his suburban land meant that George controlled the coastal land on both sides of the jetty. He was well placed for the shearing of other settlers' sheep, which he undertook for one penny a head. He had a shearing shed as early as 1854, when he records flooring it with whale bone.[18] The wool was stored in the boat shed until shipped.[19]

Provincial Councils — looking after, among other things, immigration, land administration, roading and education — were in existence in New Zealand from 1853 to 1876; the province of Marlborough was established in 1859. 'Mr Fyffe's House, Kaikouras' was listed as one of the two polling places in the Clarence Electoral District in 1862; the other was 'the Schoolhouse, Mr Tetley's Station'.[20]

The nomination of candidates took place at Tetley's, and a poll was held only if more than the two required were nominated, an infrequent happening.

The usual representatives for the district at this time were Joseph Ward, the surveyor, and runholder C. R. Keene. However, Joseph Ward wrote to George in 1863 saying 'I wish you would join us in this Council — Keene, it was fixed, was to ask you and let us know as he is going. It would be well if you could.'[21] George was nominated at Tetley's early in 1864 and returned without opposition.[22] In the August 1865 election, however, Ward and Keene were once more returned unopposed.[23] By the time the next election was held, Kai Kõura had a courthouse and elections were held there.

By the following year George was in financial difficulties. In 1855 he had applied for the lease of the Puhi Puhi Run (also known as George Fyffe's Run), the licence for which was granted in 1856. This was transferred to A. W. and H. A. Ingles and C. Pasley in 1863 and renamed the Kincaid Run. He bought nearly 7,413 hectares of the Kahu Tara Run in that year from the executors of the estate,[24] and in 1865 was advanced £8,000 by the trustees, repayable at 10% interest. This was evidently an unwise move. He went to the West Coast to look for land, but was unsuccessful, and also failed to find a market for his sheep, possibly because of the prevalence of sheep scab in Marlborough.[25] He thought of trying to find a buyer to take up a half interest in the run, but seems to have had no success here either, and in 1866 the Kahu Tara Run was sold to F. and G. F. Bullen.[26]

George tried to find ways of making a living from his Kai Kõura land — a brewery, a mill, a general store were possibilities, though his friend, runholder J. S. Caverhill, felt there were not enough people in Kai Kõura to support these ventures and advised him to drain the property and let it.[27] Less than three months later, however, George Fyffe was dead. A report in the *Evening Post,* noting that George Fyffe was well known in Wellington, went on:

> George Fyffe Esq, who has been in delicate health, as well as occasionally suffering from aberration of mind, for sometime past, suddenly came to his death in the following circumstances. His health being worse than usual, and his mind affected during the whole of the day, when, shortly after nine o'clock in the evening he was heard by his cook — George Allan — to leave the house, taking a direction towards the wharf, which is about 50 yards distant. Allan almost immediately afterwards followed him, although he could see nothing of him . . . but heard a cry that sounded like 'help'. He searched about the wharf, and afterwards fetched James Lynch, who resides near. Lynch then took a boat and went off to the schooner Ruby . . . and brought back with him George Carr, a sailor, to assist in the search, when, on coming near the wharf they saw by the light of the lantern which they had in the boat, the body of the unfortunate gentleman floating upwards in the water in the midst of some kelp.

George Fyffe second from right with the Ingles brothers and a whaler holding baby, 1860s.
(Kai Kōura Museum)

On taking it into the boat they tried means to resuscitate it, but life was extinct. There was a contused wound across the nose and eyes as if from a blow or a fall against something hard. It is surmised that while wandering on the wharf he through some cause, fell off, and in falling off his head struck against one of the iron stays at the wharf, which caused the wound and killed him. An inquest was held before H. A. Ingles, J. P. on the 4th inst, when a verdict of 'Accidental death by falling off the wharf at Kaikoura, while in an unsound state of mind' was returned by the jury. The deceased gentleman was much respected, and his death is deeply regretted by all in the neighborhood. His body was interred on the 8th instant.[28]

FIVE

Fyffe's House

George Fyffe seems to have considered Kai Kōura, rather than Kahu Tara, his home, though it was some time before he found anyone to share it with him. In October 1859 Catherine Douglas Fyfe[1] had arrived in Wellington,[2] later travelling to Kai Kōura, and she was married to George in March 1860.[3] We do not know whether they were related, but it is possible they were and that George asked her to come out. He had referred in his diary in 1855 to Cecilia whom he asked to join him, but she evidently was not willing — perhaps because he sent her an account of the 1855 earthquake in Wellington.[4] His sister Margaret had come to keep house for him, but she soon married a Wellington boat builder, John McLean, who had been George's manager at Kahu Tara. The arrival of Catherine must have been eagerly awaited by George. He was educated and considered himself a gentleman; apart from a few distant runholders and travellers he had little of what he called 'civilised' company.[5]

The cottage George and Catherine lived in was not always called 'Fyffe House'; for most of its life it had no name. The name 'Fyffe House' was given to it in recent years because it was originally the Fyffe's, and was referred to in the 1860s as Mr Fyffe's house. Later it was known as Mr Goodall's, and then Granny Low's. Its origin as a two-roomed cooper's cottage has been discussed above. It is believed that the two-storeyed wing was built in anticipation of George and Catherine's marriage; it was certainly complete, and little different from its appearance today, by 1863.[6] The floor of the two-storeyed (west) wing is lower than the much earlier cooper's wing; it has some whale bone piles, together with piles of local mudstone and limestone. That it is not completely on whale bone piles may reflect the decrease in the capture of whales.

A picket fence bounded the verandah, and by 1867 a post and rail fence marked the boundary of the section.[7] It is possible that the kitchen and the first floor area above it were built before the rest of the west wing, as a separate structure.[8] Detached kitchens were quite common as, with wooden buildings and open hearths, fires were an ever-present danger. The kitchen still contains the brick bread oven, which possibly supplied the bread for the whaling station.

Other structures, which have not survived, included a storehouse (behind the present day garage), an outhouse near the road, a large shed or cottage with a chimney (possibly the chimney which can still be seen across the road from Fyffe House) and boat sheds towards Fyffe Cove.[9] The boat sheds may be those shown on Norman's survey of 1852. The landscape seems to have been little altered from Norman's description (p.18). Part of the site was swampy; the rest appears to have been grassed; there were no trees.[10]

The house is built of pit-sawn native timbers: kahikatea, tōtara, mātai and rimu. Miro has also been used for some studs and flooring. This was not in common use for framing and it may reflect the fact that there was little timber available locally. The cavity of the timber

Fyffe House in 1863.
(From an original painting owned by the Macmillan family, Christchurch)

Fyffe house in 1867.
(Kai Kōura Museum Archives)

frame is packed with an earth/straw mix. This technique of providing insulation and fire protection was not uncommon in Canterbury, though remaining examples are scarce. Although the house is sheltered from the south winds, it would have been cold in the winter when the mountains were fully snow-covered, and insulation was sensible. The roof was probably still shingled, and the exterior was finished with pink paint, believed to have been made from red lead, white lead and whale oil. Traces of this paint remain on what was an outside wall, inside the visitors' toilet.

The interior construction was of lath — made of imported Australian eucalyptus — and plaster, finished with a fine pigmented lime plaster over base coats reinforced with animal hair. The parlour was a pale green, with woodwork grained to imitate oak; the room next door (possibly a dining room) was left white, with grey painted woodwork and ceiling. One of the bedrooms upstairs was blue, one green, and the third, over the kitchen, and which originally had open, whitewashed rafters, was tinted with red ochre to give a deep pinkish tone. The hall was probably whitewashed, possibly with a yellow ochre base, and the balustrades were finished in black with a tar-based paint.[11]

The traditional plastering methods and materials have been used to replicate the original decorative schemes in the downstairs rooms, as the later wallpapered finishes were in such poor condition that their

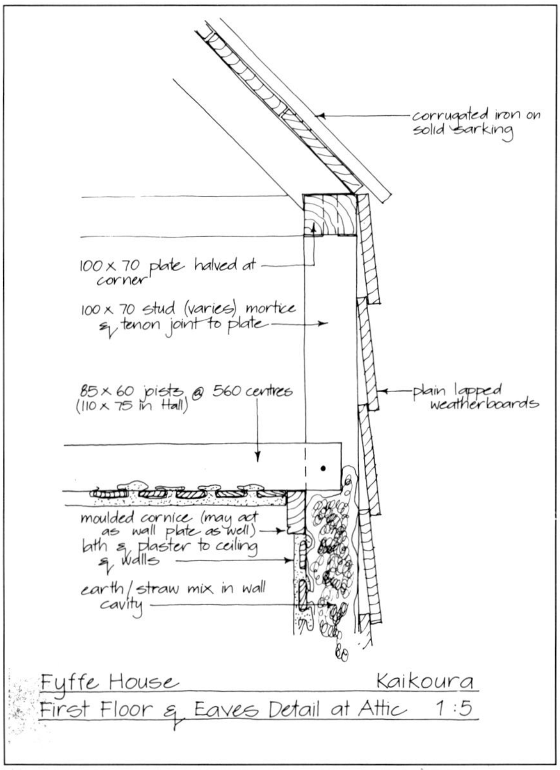

Construction details, showing earth/straw insulation. *(Diagram Chris Cochran)*

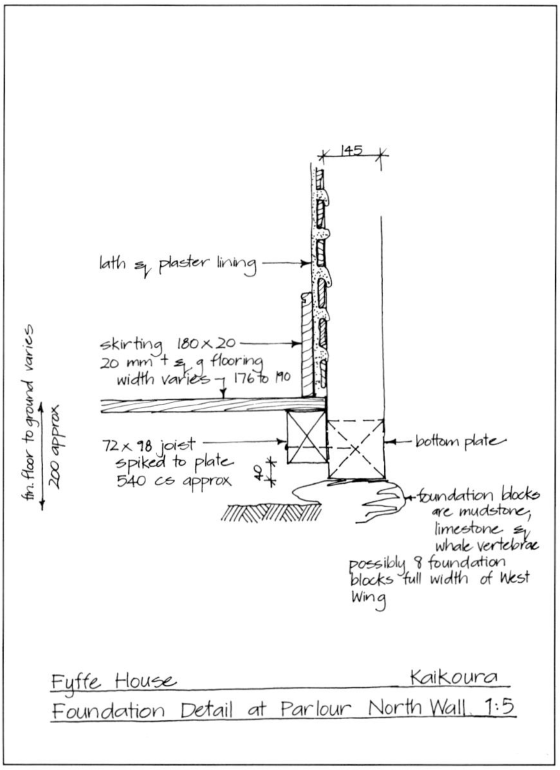

The lath and plaster lining. *(Diagram Chris Cochran)*

conservation was not feasible. Two of the bedrooms are also still plastered, a finish which seems to have been used throughout the entire occupancy of the house. The plaster in these two rooms was repaired in 1984.

Graining, as used in the parlour, was a painted finish, imitating polished timber, often oak or mahogany. This technique was in common use at this time to imitate more expensive timbers, and both graining and another painted imitative finish, marbling, were essential skills for Victorian (and earlier) painters. The graining was usually covered with two coats of varnish, which gave a durable and easy to clean finish. The paint was mixed to one's requirements, not bought ready made, and George Fyffe recorded some recipes in his notebook:

> Mahogany colour — white ground
> Brown amber and red lead — mix amber first not oil
> then add red led till the colur suit —
> oak — white ground
> mix Spanish Brown with oil
> if too dark add a little white lead
> For doors and windows
>
> Buy 2lbs Spanish Brown }
> " 3lbs amber } @ 6/- per lb
> " 2lbs red lead }
> 14 galls oil or so @ 7/- per gall.[12]

The oil would probably have been whale oil; 'amber' would be umber, darker and more brown than ochre.

We do not know how the rooms in the cooper's wing were finished as the original linings have been replaced. Nor do we know how the house was furnished. Many settlers had minimal furniture, often that which they had used on the voyage out, such as folding chairs. They often made necessary items such as benches and shelves, and trunks and boxes could serve as seats, tables or storage facilities as needed. Further storage was provided by pegs or nails on the walls. The floors might be covered with oilcloth, matting or a carpet according to means and availability.

Lighting would at first have included lamps burning whale oil, as well as candles. Kerosene would eventually have replaced whale oil, probably in the 1860s. Cooking — apart from food cooked in the bread oven — was probably still done over an open fire.

The parlour was usually a 'best' room, used only on formal occasions. Standard furniture included a central table, usually circular and covered with a heavy cloth, several upright chairs, one or more armchairs, and perhaps a sofa. Additional items might have included a bookcase, a writing table or desk, and a piano. This is something we know Catherine possessed.

A travelling Marist priest, Father Garin, recorded:

> It was on the Sunday evening the 9th of March 1861 that I arrived at Mr Fife's station, where I was received with much cordiality by Mr and Mrs Fife. Mr Jos Ward and his son Master Austin had come with me as guides. Here I hear that Mr Butt is expected for tomorrow Sunday when he will hold service at Mr Fife's. I sleep in the room which had been prepared for him.
>
> On Sunday morning, as Mr Butt has not arrived, Mrs Fife asks me to hold a service in the large room; but I observe that Mr Butt might come and as nearly all those present are protestants, it might inconvenience the Rev. Gentleman; she answers that as he has not come I was quite justified in taking the precedence. She says she will assist at my prayer and will play pieces on the piano. She offers to sing with playing but I remark that as she has perhaps not got Catholic pieces, I will be satisfied with the playing: Agreed. Catholics present are Messrs Ward Jos., Ward Austin, Wickman, Rily and another. All the others are protestants, the house is full. I say the Catholic prayers after having begun by the Sign of the Cross; I give an instruction in English to the English portion, and in Maori to the Maori. After service is over Mr Butt arrives. We proceed to take dinner; the Rev. Mr Butt and Father Garin fraternizing. Towards evening Mrs Fife asks Austin if he will not go to their service at 6 o'clock? to which Austin replies without hesitation: No Certainly Mam. They have their service at 6 o'clock and we at the same hour, in another room; but at the same time enjoying the music which was not, however, intended for us . . .[13]

Māori missionaries visited Kai Kōura in the 1840s, and Chief Kai Kōura Whakatau conducted prayers at his settlement at Mikonui.[14] The Rev. Butt had been visiting occasionally since 1858, and other Anglican priests passed through, holding services or baptisms at the Fyffe's and enjoying 'the magnificent Kaikouras as seen from your house across the bay . . . your kind hospitality'.[15] Father Garin's was the first Catholic service in Kai Kōura, and a Presbyterian minister did not visit until 1864.[16] It is possible that Robert Fyfe held prayers at his Wai ō Puka whaling station, as he had obtained an 1849 edition of the Presbyterian *Confession of Faith,* containing also the Catechisms, Covenant and Directory of Publick Worship. This, the only artefact of his which has survived, is now on display at Fyffe House.

Church services seem to have been a fairly rare occurrence; there were, however, other social gatherings, particularly for men. On 2 July 1862 an accommodation house was opened in Kai Kōura. Named The Traveller's Rest, it was operated by Joseph Charleston, a former whaler and shepherd.[17] An accommodation house or hotel has stood on the site since that date. Accommodation houses were usually simple structures providing food and shelter for travellers and their horses. They were licensed to sell alcoholic liquor and so became social centres in the districts they served. The Traveller's Rest seems mostly to have been referred to as Charleston's; it catered for whalers, seamen, shepherds and other farm workers, and visiting runholders too.[18] Within George Fyffe's lifetime the little settlement grew large enough to support two more hostelries — the Caledonian Hotel and the Kaikoura Hotel (and brewery) — both built in 1865;[19] a Post Office (the mail arrived fortnightly), a courthouse, and a schoolhouse (all 1866) and a store (1867).[20]

There are few references to women at Kai Kōura at this time, and probably there were few congenial female companions for Catherine. One was a Mrs McInnes, whose husband worked for George and later went into business for himself. Mrs McInnes seems to have been housekeeper for George Fyffe before Catherine's arrival and may have continued helping afterwards.[21] There are no references to maidservants, and servants were difficult to obtain in New Zealand. However, it is possible that whalers' daughters might have been employed for housework and laundry and possibly for cooking, although the Fyffes probably shared the services of their (male) station cooks.

Catherine seems to have become involved in community life. For example, she was called upon late in 1864 to set the broken arm of Sarah Ann Riley at Rangi nui wai (also known as Riley's Fishery), several kilometres south of Kai Kōura. This implies either that there were few other women to call on, or perhaps that Catherine had more medical knowledge than anyone else available locally. It was not until some time after her death that there were enough settlers to raise a subscription for a resident doctor.[22]

Catherine was evidently fond of animals and brought a dog and cat with her to New Zealand. Her interest in music extended to opera; a list of stores wanted in 1863 included 'Faust by Gounod with an English version of the music and the principal airs'.[23] This was first performed in Paris in 1859, the year Catherine sailed for New Zealand. The stores also included the seeds of parsley, mustard and cress; fresh greens would have been a welcome addition to the basic meat and potato diet. No doubt other vegetables were grown — the garden was beside the road[24] — but we do not know whether Catherine had a flower garden. Fruit trees, referred to in diaries, seem to have been planted at Kahu Tara, not Kai Kōura.

Catherine and George had no children, and when she died on 8 August 1868 all of their effects were sold, George having died intestate and in debt.[25] They were not entirely forgotten, however, as three years later their friend Caverhill was arranging for their graves in Kai Kōura Cemetery to be fenced and sending 'some choice seeds . . . from Hawkswood for the purpose of improving that part of the cemetery . . . [and he] on a former occasion caused some shrubs to be planted near the graves'.[26]

SIX

Kai Kōura Becomes a Port

THE FYFFE'S HOUSE was bought by Joseph Wilkinson Goodall. Born in Staffordshire in 1835, he had arrived in New Zealand with his brother Samuel in about 1860. They joined the Constabulary, Samuel in Havelock and Joseph in Nelson. Joseph was transferred to Kai Kōura in 1865, taking over from a district constable appointed in 1863, who had been unable to control the alcohol-related disorder in the settlement. Joseph succeeded within months where his predecessor had failed, and the following year he was made sergeant,[1] at 9/- a day; a constable was paid 8/6d.[2] £100 was provided in the 1864-65 Provincial Estimates for building a lockup at Kai Kōura, which was in place by 1869, probably earlier;[3] a courthouse with stables for the constabulary horses was built in 1866.

The Courthouse did not meet with universal approval; £250 had been allowed and this was apparently exceeded, causing one irate taxpayer to complain that the Council should provide a better road instead of a 'temple of Justice' where the magistrate sat only once a month. The anonymous resident went on to complain at the 'common constable' collecting the education rate 'tricked out in all the brutalising insignia of his man-hunting calling'[4] — that is, revolver and handcuffs.

The cases dealt with by the constable appear to have been minor ones and were frequently to do with infringements of the Licensing Act — liquor had long been a major import into Kai Kōura. Goodall's most serious case concerned the death of Sarah Ann Riley. She and her husband Bernard (Barney) lived next door to his brother James and his Māori wife. When Sarah Ann died in 1865 James Riley was held on suspicion of manslaughter (he was said to have punched her over the eye and hit her over the head with a tea tray). However, in the absence of confirming medical opinion as to the cause of death he was discharged, the jury returning an open verdict. The editorial in the *Marlborough Press* castigated almost everyone concerned, and suggested

The Seaward Kai Kōuras *(Grant Sheehan)*

The view from Takahanga. *(Grant Sheehan)*

Maru Kai Tātea at Takahanga. *(Grant Sheehan)*

Harpoon heads at Kai Kōura Museum. *(Grant Sheehan)*

A trypot outside Kai Kōura Museum. *(Grant Sheehan)*

The old wharf. *(Grant Sheehan)*

The old chimney. *(Grant Sheehan)*

The old wharf near Fyffe House – the whaling station was to the left of the photograph. *(Grant Sheehan)*

The parlour with restored plaster walls and grained woodwork. *(Photograph by the author)*

The bread oven in the kitchen. *(Grant Sheehan)*

One of the whale bone piles. *(Grant Sheehan)*

One of the 19th century locks. *(Grant Sheehan)*

The staircase. *(Grant Sheehan)*

The front bedroom.
(Grant Sheehan)

Furnishings in the front bedroom. The framed text is a Band of Hope pledge signed by Fred Low.
(Grant Sheehan)

A frieze which was discovered in what is now the sales room. The nautical theme is very appropriate. *(Stephen Cashmore)*

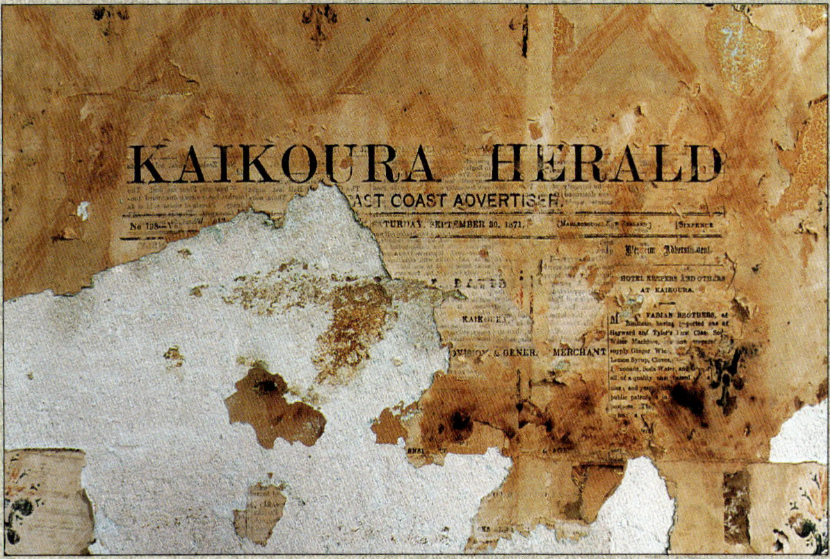

The newspaper patch. *(Stephen Cashmore)*

The brown paper patch. *(Stephen Cashmore)*

The first wallpaper in the parlour. *(Stephen Cashmore)*

Fyffe House by day ...

... and by night. *(Both photographs by Grant Sheehan)*

that the matter had been hushed up, or that such crimes were 'too common at the Kaikoras to call for more than a passing notice'.[5]

After James Riley died in 1870 his brother Barney evidently felt it was safe to marry again and in due course placed a notice in the *Kaikoura Herald and East Coast Advertiser:*

> NOTICE TO LADIES
> Wanted a wife. A widow preferred. A good home and a loving husband. Apply to B. Riley. Riley's Fishery.[6]

Joseph Goodall. *(NZHPT)*

Although he advertised for several weeks he was not successful, and eventually became a well-known and colourful visitor to Kai Kōura's hotels. His clothes were patched with flour bags, his hat was decorated with flowers from the gardens he passed, and he muttered threats against those he disliked as he walked along, or stopped to argue with a tree. He was frequently fined or briefly imprisoned for drunkenness, but this did not alter his unvarying habits. Eventually, in 1904, he was removed to a home in Wellington.[7]

At Rangi nui wai whaling had ceased after the death of James Riley. Wai ō Puka closed after the death of George Fyffe (though it had virtually ceased long before); a whaling party was based there from 1874 to 1878, but this was the last. Some whalers, at least, remained permanently: two European graves on the hill above the whaling station were noted by Joseph Ward in his survey, and are presumed to be the graves of whalers.[8] The South Bay whaling station was auctioned in 1869.[9] For the rest of the nineteenth century small parties came to South Bay only in the winter. They hunted sperm whales and humpbacks, the latter being more numerous than sperm whales, but much more difficult and dangerous to catch.

European settlement in Kai Kōura had begun with whaling and then looked inland to sheep farming. However, the sea was always a most important element. So important was it that in 1863 one newspaper editor felt that Kai Kōura was really part of Wellington rather than Marlborough, as it was the sea link to Wellington which was relied upon.[10] By the end of 1866 a bridle track had been formed all the way along the coast, but the *Kaikoura Herald and East Coast Advertiser* in 1869 complained that 'there is scarce a single mile of formed road which is passable for laden drays',[11] and again in 1871 that 'not a single chain of road has ever been metalled in this county that we are aware of and not a single creek of any moment has been bridged'.[12]

In response to petitions from the residents, Kai Kōura was gazetted a port of entry in July 1869, with W. H. Pilliet as customs officer. The chimney across the road from Fyffe House is believed to be all that remains of the bonded warehouse, or custom house as it was known

The Police Station and Post & Telegraph Office, 1873. *(Kai Kōura Museum)*

locally. This building, with no chimney in evidence, appears in several late nineteenth and early twentieth century photographs. It is possible that this was the cottage or shed present in the sketches of the 1860s. The harbour master was E. G. T. Gooch, who had built a boiling-down works near the beach at Kai Kōura. This establishment, named the next year the Kaikoura Tallow and Soap Works, was an attempt to make use of surplus stock which were difficult to sell owing to sheep scab in Marlborough.[13]

Other businesses at this time included a flour mill,[14] a branch of the Post Office Savings Bank, a bricklayer and limeburner, a builder, contractor and undertaker, a saddler and harnessmaker, a tailor, a boot- and shoemaker, a wheelwright and carpenter, a chemist, a printery with newspaper — the *Kaikoura Herald and East Coast Advertiser* — and another store. The two latter were short-lived; the newspaper ran from 1868-72 and the store lasted for a few months. Kai Kōura was too small to support two stores, and the first store had the advantage of being owned by Captain Davidson, who also owned the 25-ton schooner *Ruby*, which was Kai Kōura's regular ship from 1863-75.[15]

Exports were potatoes, wool, bacon and limestone. Imports included timber, fencing wire, basic stores (flour, oatmeal, sugar, tea, salt, raisins, candles and kerosene), tobacco (for sheep dip as well as smoking) and very large quantities of liquor.[16]

While one must assume that drinking was the predominant leisure activity, there were others. Church services were held in the court house and school house, and a Catholic church had been opened in

1868.[17] The first Anglican church, St James, was opened in 1873 at the Kōwhai, followed by St Peter's in the town. The church at the Kōwhai is still standing, in Red Swamp Road. Joseph Goodall was a member of the building committee for it and later a churchwarden.

A circulating library was operating from the beginning of 1870 (and the mails from this year were delivered once a week); there were public meetings and dinners, race meetings at South Bay, cricket matches, and an occasional ball — at one in 1871 there were all of twelve women present.[18] A couple of weeks later a photographer visited Kai Kōura, which must have excited no little interest.

While photographs of the little settlement reveal it as bleak and treeless in the 1870s, the *Kaikoura Herald and East Coast Advertiser* offered monthly garden notes — principally mentioning vegetables, herbs and fruit, but also a few flowers and shrubs. Roses, rosemary, lavender, fuchsias, mignonette, hollyhocks, dahlias, chrysanthemums, marigolds, pinks, carnations, sweet william, stocks, geraniums, cockscomb, balsam, amaranthus and sweet peas are mentioned in September-October. The newspaper, noting that most settlers had confined their tree planting to poplar, willow and Australian gums and wattles as the easiest to grow, also made a plea for the planting of mulberry trees so that silk worms could be cultivated.[19] New industries were constantly being sought; flax growing was one which was fre-

Margaret Goodall. *(NZHPT)*

The port area in c.1887 with *Wakatu* in foreground and Fyffe House at left. *(Kai Kōura Museum)*

quently advocated but, like silkworms, it does not appear to have been tried.

In order to make a living, settlers frequently had to turn their hands to a variety of occupations, and Joseph Goodall is an example of this. He became Clerk of the Court on leaving the Constabulary,[20] then the following year added the roles of Registrar of Births, Deaths and Marriages, Returning and Registration Officer, Officer in Charge of H. M. Customs and Licensing Officer.[21]

In 1876 Joseph married Margaret Daniel Duncan (c.1856-1896), daughter of a sawmiller, Alexander Scott Duncan, and his wife Elizabeth Daniel. Within a few years Joseph had changed his occupation again, becoming the first wharf manager.[22] In 1879 the port had been visited by 136 ships — the maximum it was to achieve. Something more than a small jetty was required, and by 1881 — with a government grant of £1,000 — a wharf was completed and a cargo shed built. The wharf, on the site of the old jetty, was practically next door to Fyffe House. In 1883 the port was handed over to the Kaikoura County Council, which sat as the Harbour Board, but declining trade caused the abolition of the Harbour Board in 1887.[23]

By 1907 a new wharf was needed, and was constructed nearer the town, where it still stands, having been opened in 1909. The old wharf continued to be used by professional fishermen for many years. It was shortened — against the wishes of local fishermen[24] — and can still be seen across the road from Fyffe House.

The wharf area in 1908, with (from left) customs shed, hotel stables, Pier Hotel, Goodall's wharf shed, Fyffe House, Council wharf shed. *(Kai Kōura Museum)*

In 1885 Joseph had the Pier Hotel built on the Fyffe House section and leased it to a series of licensed proprietors. Between the hotel and Fyffe House stood his large shed or warehouse, and on the corner of the property, beside the road, were the hotel's stables. The hotel was cut into sections in 1909 and moved nearer to the new wharf, where it still stands, being known locally as the fishermen's hotel. The original foundations of the hotel and the shed (which was still standing in 1915) can be seen in the grounds of Fyffe House.

The house in the Goodalls' time, c.1896. *(NZHPT)*

Joseph and Margaret Goodall made few changes to Fyffe House; the main change to the exterior was the enclosure of one section of the verandah with corrugated iron to form a small room. This was used by Joseph Goodall as an office, presumably after he became wharf manager. It was possibly at this time that the roof was covered with corrugated iron. It seems to have been the Goodalls who first made a flower garden in the area enclosed by the two wings of the house. This space was defined by a white picket fence that continued as a board fence along the verandah. The angles between the verandah and its posts were decorated (this had disappeared by the 1930s) and there were finials on the gables. The small garden had colourful borders and included two lilac bushes, a magnolia, rose and honeysuckle.[25] A fence and a line of boxthorn and macrocarpa trees (now gone) marked the front boundary of the section, and a board fence separated the house from the hotel.[26] Boxthorn survives behind the house and is now classed as a noxious weed.

During the Goodall's occupancy, wallpaper was used for the first time. It is assumed that this happened when Joseph married Margaret Goodall in 1876. It was certainly installed in the parlour after 1871, because between the glaze which covered the original lime plaster and the first wallpaper the plaster was patched with a piece of brown wrapping paper inscribed:

> On Public Service Only
> Officer-in-Charge
> Kaikoura.

The postmark is Wellington, August 31, 1871. Another part of the wall contained a patch from the *Kaikoura Herald and East Coast Advertiser* of Saturday 30 September, 1871.

This parlour wallpaper was typical of the 1870s. It is a trellis design with stylised motifs in several colours on a natural ground. The cupboard was left unpapered and was lined with bookshelves. In the room next door — now the sales room — the first wallpaper had flower clusters on a white ground with blue dots. This paper had been varnished at some stage. The upstairs bedroom over the kitchen was lined with boards and scrim and wallpaper applied. Here the first paper was

The Pier Hotel, c.1905.
(Kai Kōura Museum)

also a floral design, in grey and white on cream. These rooms were repapered over the years, the last papers being of the 1920s. Samples of successive wallpapers and paint finishes used in the parlour and sales room can be seen on display in the house.

Like the Fyffes, and in common with most houses at this time, the Goodalls had no bathroom. The male Goodalls are said to have bathed each day in a salt water bath formed by the rocks across the road. The women presumably bathed in the kitchen, which has been described as whitewashed, with dark beams and a fireplace the length of the wall;[27] it is probable that a range was installed in the fireplace — next to the old bread oven — in the 1870s or 1880s. Water was supplied from a tank to the west of the house, beside the kitchen.

Margaret Goodall died in 1896, ten days after the birth of a son, and Joseph died in 1911. They had five sons (one of whom died before Joseph) and three daughters, so during their occupancy Fyffe House was a family home for the first time. The executors of the estate — William Duncan, Alexander Duncan Goodall, Charlotte Elizabeth Goodall and Edward Goodall — decided to subdivide and sell Section 224 and a plan was finally approved in 1920.[28]

SEVEN

Fishing and Self-sufficiency

SECTION 224 was divided into five lots. Lot 1, containing Fyffe House, was sold in 1920 to James Johnston, a settler who had operated the Clarence Bridge Accommodation House. In 1922 the property passed to his son, James Allen (Jimmy) Johnston.[1] A whaler, he had built a whaling factory at South Bay.

Whaling was now very different from the early days. A. D. Goodall (son of Joseph) and his partner W. Kinley had been the first to depart from traditional methods when they had a boat specially built in 1908 and fitted it with a muzzle-loading harpoon gun and bomb gun. Jimmy Johnston bought two fast launches — the *Sussex* and the *Peerless* — in 1917, specially designed and built in Picton, outfitted with harpoon guns and electrically detonated hand bombs. The South Bay factory was equipped with a traction engine to haul up the whales — mainly humpbacks — and there were mechanical slicers and large vats instead of trypots.[2]

Six humpback and three right whales were brought in during the first season, nine humpbacks in the second and 11 in the third. Jimmy Johnston acquired a launch, *Kersage,* in 1920 from noted boatbuilder Ernie Lane of Picton, and Arthur Jackson and L. Traill came from Picton with the *Swiftsure.*[3] Twenty humpbacks and one sperm whale were caught in 1920 and the following year 16 humpbacks and two right whales. However the income was absorbed by the expense of damage to the chasers, which had been driven on shore by southerly storms, and the factory closed in 1922, Johnston having abandoned whaling the year before. He was involved in many other ventures, principally contracting, including road construction and bridge building. Jimmy was a Kaikoura County Councillor, involved in many local sporting organisations, and served for 25 years on the District High School Committee.[4]

From the 1880s the steamer *Wakatu* (157 tons) was the regular ship on the east coast run. In the early hours of 6 September 1924 the

Jimmy Johnston and Gwen Low, granddaughter of Maud and Joseph.
(Low family)

Wakatu grounded at Wai Papa Point near Kai Kōura and lay on the beach for 30 years. Eventually the hull was sold as scrap metal by Jimmy Johnston. By the time the *Wakatu* grounded, Kai Kōura's shipping trade was again in decline, and the County Council closed the wharf and sheds in 1931.

The Johnstons did not live in Fyffe House, but Jimmy Johnston seems to have used part of the site as a loading area. The house was occupied by Joseph and Maud Low and their eight children. Joseph, born in Scotland in 1856, was a sailor who 'jumped ship' in Kai Kōura, and there he married Maud Flint (the Flints were a local fishing family). At first they lived across the road from Fyffe House, but were living in Fyffe House at least by the 1920s, probably earlier. Joseph bought Lots 2-5 — the balance of the original Section 224 — in 1920.[5] On his death in 1928 these portions passed to his widow. Jimmy Johnston sold Lot 1 in 1935 to Joseph Soutar, a nephew of Joseph Low. Soutar served in the United States army during the Spanish-American War of 1898 and then in the Philippines; he came to New Zealand in 1921. After Joseph Low's death, Maud continued to live in Fyffe House (then known as 'Granny Low's'), while Soutar lived in a small cottage or bach on the site, and when he died in 1943 he left the property to her, thus uniting Section 224 once more.[6]

Joseph Low.
(Low family)

Joseph Soutar's bach.
(NZHPT)

Fishing was always a way of earning a livelihood in Kai Kōura, but it was not very profitable (fishing at this time meant wet fishing — that is, not crayfishing). A Kaikoura Refrigeration and Fishing Company, which operated from Joseph Goodall's large shed, was not a success due to defective machinery; it existed from 1906 to 1910. Feron and Son's cooling plant erected at the old wharf in 1916 was a more profitable operation.[7] The water for the freezers was pumped to a concrete reservoir on the wharf from a well on a corner of the Low's property.[8] The old wharf was used by the fishermen, and on Sundays everyone, including farmers from the surrounding district, gathered there to barter for fish. Crayfish and wet fish were cheap and plentiful then. The export of crayfish tails in the 1960s to America was a successful venture which made crayfish an expensive luxury for New Zealanders.

Maud and two of her grandchildren in the garden. *(Low family)*

Both Joseph Low and his nephew were described as fishermen, though they were not full-time commercial fishermen. Joseph Low, a small red-bearded man, also worked on the wharf unloading boats, and kept a few hens, pigs and about 20 cows; these provided milk, cream, home-made butter and a cheque from the dairy, which was the family's main source of income. The cows were milked by Maud, who also had a large vegetable garden on a rise to the west of Fyffe House. This not only fed the family but provided a surplus to swap with other families.[9] The 'east enders' as the families at this end of Kai Kōura were known, were a close-knit community, many of them related. They shared the little they had, and the children played and swam together. Everyone knew Maud — 'Granny Low' — with her long black dresses, boots and walking stick. She was considered strict and was respected by the local children.[10]

In the Lows' time the kitchen was the heart of the house, where the family lived. It was a cosy room, with the black range going, and a cup of tea and Granny's home baking were always offered. Electric light was installed in the kitchen in the mid 1930s — it had been supplied to the west end of Kai Kōura in 1922 — but electricity was too expensive for cooking or for the rest of the house. A piano stood in front of where the old brick bread oven had been, there was a dresser with good china, a couch and Granny Low's special chair. A large table was used for family meals and afterward the washing up basin was brought out of the pantry and the dishes done on the table.

Water came from two tanks — a second one had been installed in the garden, in the angle of the house. Everyone who could afford it had two tanks, and sometimes a well. Hot water was supplied from the coal range with its brass tap, and on Sunday nights the children bathed in a tin bath in front of the fire.

By the 1930s the parlour and the room next to it (now the sales room) were unfurnished and unused, though the parlour at least had been repapered in the 1920s.[11] Maud slept in the cooper's wing; some

Maud and hens.
(Low family)

of her furniture can now be seen in other parts of the house. The adjoining room in that wing was the girls' room, later used by visiting family. The boys slept upstairs, with George Low by himself in the front upstairs bedroom overlooking the sea. It is believed that George, the baby of the family, fell into a well when very young — an accident from which he never fully recovered.

Maud Low was said to be a hard-working woman, and after Joseph's death she continued to run the property. She made her own soap, hooked rag rugs for the polished floors, cured bacon and ham, milked the cows and tended the garden. Photographs of the time show the verandah was edged with a healthy grape vine growing up wire netting. There was no longer a picket fence (this was replaced by a wire one), and Maud had a cottage garden. The rest of the property was pasture for the cows, which were milked in a cowshed up the hill near the vegetable garden. Here, too, were the pigsties, hen house and the hay shed. In the middle of the front pasture was a large macrocarpa tree, with a row of them forming the front boundary. Many of these were blown away in a big nor'-wester storm, which also took away a hen house — hens and all. They were never seen again.

EIGHT

The Return of the Whales

THERE WERE MANY CHANGES after the Second World War. Maud died in 1951, leaving the house to her youngest child, George. She had been predeceased by two of her sons — Fred, who died of cancer, and Doug, who was drowned. His boat overturned by the reef off Kai Kõura and his body was never recovered; one of the many lives lost in New Zealand coastal waters.[1]

After his mother's death George continued the self-sufficient lifestyle, keeping cows, hens, and sheep — which he butchered himself in the back porch. He also went out regularly after crayfish, using crayfish pots he 'knitted' himself in the kitchen. After he had retired from fishing, his boat, which was built by Ernie Lane, lay in the parlour of Fyffe House for many years. It is now stored under cover behind the garage.

Few changes were made in the house by George. He closed off the cooper's wing and seems to have inhabited mainly the kitchen and his bedroom, using the rest of the house for storage. He installed the enamel coal range in the kitchen in the 1960s, together with a hot water cylinder, a bath and tubs in the room next door, and a water closet in the room off the verandah. This is now the visitors' toilet.

George was said to be odd, and of impaired intellectual capacity because of his fall down the well when very young. He was, however, said to be a shrewd bargainer who spent little and built up considerable wealth. Much of this he left as a trust fund to the County Council. A moody and quick-tempered man, he had few friends. His sister Bessie Oldman, who used to come and help her mother in the house, also visited daily to clean for her brother George and help with the milking until her death in 1972. However, by the later 1970s the house was rapidly deteriorating, and George would not repair it. The local Regional Committee of the New Zealand Historic Places Trust brought the house to the attention of the Trust's head office in Wellington.

George Low in the kitchen. *(Low family)*

George in his boat, 1930s.

Fyffe House in the 1950s. *(Kai Kōura Museum)*

George made a will leaving the house to the Trust, which repaired the roof and walls and painted the house in its original pink tone. After George's death in 1980 the Trust had the cooper's wing repaired and redecorated as quarters for a tenant. The kitchen was upgraded with an electric stove, and electricity was installed upstairs (George had carried a candle up to bed all his life). The two plastered bedrooms — repaired in 1984 — were furnished as they would have been at around the turn of the century; much of the furniture belonged to the Lows. Lots 2-5 were sold, and in 1985 Lot 1, containing the house, was made an Historic Reserve.

The picket fence, and the paling fence along the end of the verandah, were replaced. The delightful cottage garden was recreated by Mrs Denise Harris, tenant for a decade. She also kept many animals, including hens, cats and goats, in the tradition of the former owners. In 1990 the family of Mrs Margaret Wood, who died in 1989 and was a member of a longstanding Kai Kōura family, donated $20,000 to the Historic Places Trust for conservation work at Fyffe House. A memorial service for Mrs Wood was held at the house in 1992.

The policy guiding the conservation work is the tradition of small-scale change over a long period of time, and as far as is possible all building fabric from former owners is considered to be of equal value.[2] The work involved upgrading the kitchen (including new laundry facilities), removing the bath and tubs from the sales room, inserting a new bathroom in the back porch and installing a hand basin in the outside toilet for visitors.

The paint and wallpapers were carefully examined and it was discovered that the original decorative finish was lime plaster. The condition of the wallpapers was so poor that they could not be conserved, and while the sequence of paint finishes was clear, it was not possible to tell when they were applied, or with which wallpaper. It was therefore decided to return to George Fyffe's original plaster walls and, in the parlour, his oak grained paint, traces of which had been discovered.[3] Samples of the wallpapers and paint colours are displayed so that visitors can see how later owners chose to decorate the house. Traditional techniques were used for the repair of the plaster and its finishing coat, and as much preparation as possible was done on site. The house was kept open so that visitors could observe the work as it progressed.

In the past, visitors to Kai Kõura have mostly come for seaside holidays, and to enjoy the magnificent scenery. They still come for these reasons, but since 1989 many more have come to see the whales — mainly parãoa, sperm whales. Tohorã, right whales, are increasing in numbers, but are still rare. The Kãi Tahu, who have lived in the area for over 300 years, now operate a whale watching business. The whales brought Europeans to Kai Kõura and are now bringing tourists from many countries. Many of these tourists, and many New Zealanders interested in their own history, visit Fyffe House to see Kai Kõura's earliest surviving building and the sole survivor of a vanished industry.

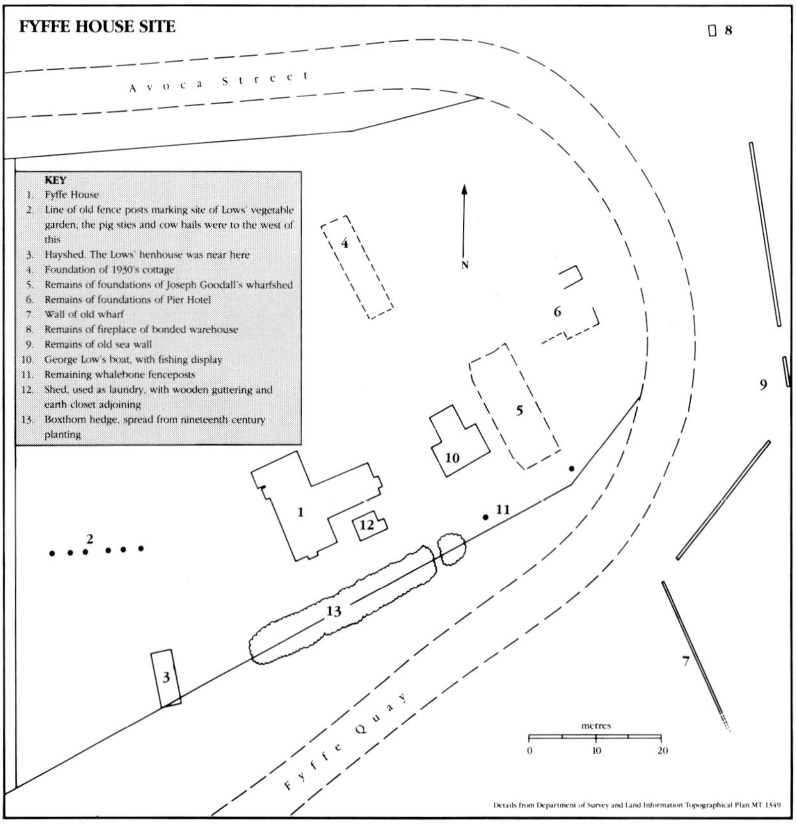

Plan of the site.
(Drawn by Tim Galloway)

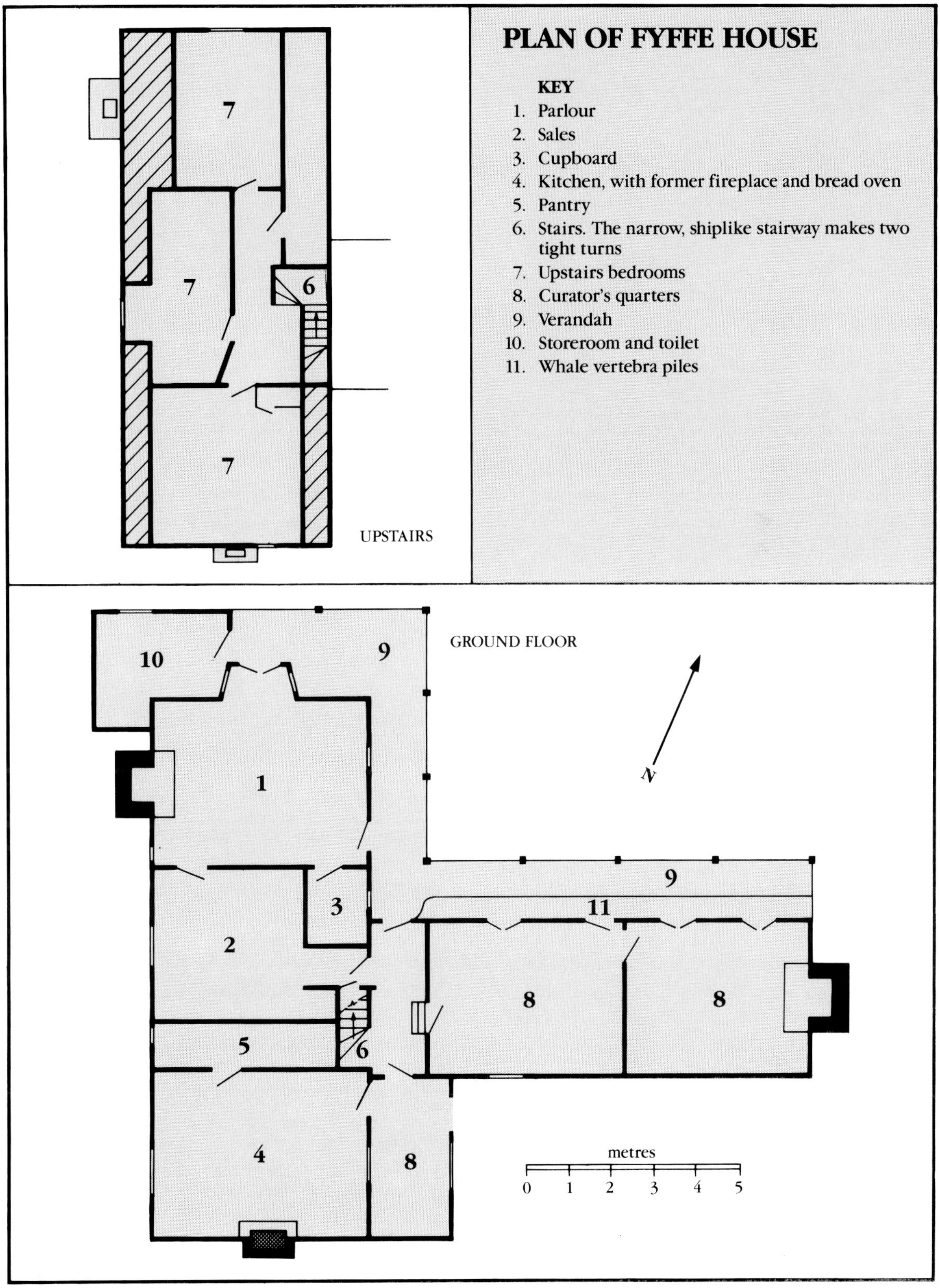

Plan of the house. *(Drawn by Tim Galloway)*

Notes

NOTES TO CHAPTER ONE

1. New Zealand Geographic Board, *He Kõrero Pũrakau mõ Ngã Taunahanahatanga a Ngã Tũpuna/Place Names of the Ancestors, A Mãori Oral History Atlas*, p. 91.
2. New Zealand Historic Places Trust file HP11004-112; Michael Trotter and Beverley McCulloch, *Unearthing New Zealand,* pp. 19-21.
3. *Lyttelton Times,* 5 August 1857.
4. Robert and George Fyffe Estate Papers: George Fyffe to Bethune & Hunter, Wellington, 20 September 1864.
5. Michael Trotter and Beverley McCulloch, *Fyffe's Revisited. Records of the Canterbury Museum*, Vol. 10, No. 7, May 1993, p. 86.
6. B. G. McFadgen, 'Beach ridges, breakers and bones: late Holocene geology and archaeology of the Fyffe site, S49/46, Kaikoura Peninsula, New Zealand', in *Journal of The Royal Society of New Zealand,* Vol.17, No. 4, 1987, pp. 381-94.
7. Te Maire Tau, Anake Goodall, David Palmer and Rakiihia Tau, *Te Whakatau Kaupapa: Ngai Tahu Resource Management Strategy for the Canterbury Region*, pp. 3.7-3.8.
8. NZHPT file HP 29015-007.
9. Anne Geelen, 'Historic Pa, Modern Marae', in *New Zealand Historic Places,* September 1992, pp. 12-13.
10. The customary date for this battle is 1828. However, Beverley McCulloch of Canterbury Museum, who has done extensive research on Te Rauparaha's southern raids, believes 1830 is the correct date.
11. NZHPT file HP 29015-007; Stephen Oliver, 'Te Rauparaha', in *New Zealand Dictionary of Biography,* Vol. 1, pp. 504-7.
12. J. M. Sherrard, *Kaikoura. A History of the District*, p. 36; Harry C. Evison, 'Kaikoura Whakatau' in *New Zealand Dictionary of Biography*, Vol. 2, pp. 251-2.
13. Sherrard, pp. 106-10.
14. Ibid. pp. 110-13.

NOTES TO CHAPTER TWO

1. Harry Morton, *The Whale's Wake,* p. 16.
2. Ibid. pp. 276-7.
3. Ibid. pp. 225-9.
4. Ibid. p. 237.
5. Ibid. pp. 77, 226.
6. Kelvin Day, *Shore Whaling,* Porirua Museum History Series No. 1, p.10.
7. Morton, pp. 51-6.
8. Ibid. p. 251.
9. Ibid. pp. 62, 254-7.
10. Ibid. pp. 253-5.
11. Ibid. pp. 305, 310.

NOTES TO CHAPTER THREE

1. There are a number of ways of spelling the name — Fiffe, Fife, Fyffe, Fyfe. This does not seem to have been standardised in the early part of the nineteenth century. Robert himself seems to have always used *Fyfe* — see Trotter and McCulloch, *Fyffe's Revisited*, pp. 73-4. Although his father was married as a *Fyffe*, Robert was baptised under the name *Fiffe* — see file at New Zealand Dictionary of Biography. George was always *Fyffe*. Robert has been referred to as *Fyffe* for most of this century by various writers, including the entry in the *New Zealand Dictionary of Biography*. I have chosen the spelling he used himself and which was used by his correspondents in the nineteenth century.
2. Don Grady, 'Fyffe, Alexander Robert', in *New Zealand Dictionary of Biography,* Vol. 1, p. 142.
3. Topographic Plan of Armers Beach, MT 1358.
4. Sherrard, p. 79.
5. Ibid. p. 58. Numbers employed declined each year; only 30 were employed in 1847. See Sherrard, pp. 66-7.
6. Fyffe-Wade Whaling Agreement 1843, cited in Sherrard, Appendix I, p. 323.

7. It appears on a survey plan of 1852, prepared by Edward Norman and now in National Archives, Wellington.
8. Chris Cochran, *Fyffe House, Kaikoura: Conservation Plan*, pp. 7-8.
9. Ibid., *Addendum*, p. 8.
10. Sherrard, p. 59; *New Zealand Gazette and Wellington Spectator*, 30 January 1844.
11. Sherrard, p. 60.
12. Ibid. pp. 76-7.
13. Ibid. p. 81; *New Zealand Spectator and Cook Strait Guardian*, 29 November 1845.
14. Morton, p. 247.
15. Sherrard, pp. 64-5.
16. A 'depasturage' licence was one which allowed stock to graze on the area under licence.
17. Sherrard, pp. 96-7.
18. Inward correspondence of the Colonial Secretary, New Munster: Norman to the Colonial Secretary, 28 November 1852.
19. Ibid.
20. Robert Fyffe Estate Papers.

NOTES TO CHAPTER FOUR

1. Robert Fyffe Estate Papers.
2. *Lyttelton Times*, 10 January 1855.
3. Robert Fyffe Estate Papers: Court Order, 22 July 1864.
4. George Fyffe's Notebook, 5 June 1854.
5. Plans for a house at Kahu Tara appear in his 1854 and 1863-64 Notebooks.
6. Apart from John McLean who became his brother-in-law, there was Robert Palmer, who was there for several years. Sherrard, p. 121; George Fyffe's Notebook, 1863.
7. George Fyffe's Day and Cash Book 1857; Sherrard, p. 89.
8. George Fyffe's Notebook, 8-9 December 1854.
9. George Fyffe's Day and Cash Book, 1857.
10. George Fyffe's Notebook, 1863-64.
11. Sherrard, pp. 70, 151.
12. Robert Fyffe Estate Papers, Account No. 1, 5 December 1855.
13. George Fyffe Papers, letter to Bethune and Hunter 6 July 1861.
14. Register of Lands Sold, p. 22, 3 April 1862.
15. Survey Office Crown Grant Book, Vol. 17, pp. 9-10.
16. Register of Lands Sold, p. 52, 29 February 1864.
17. Sherrard, p. 231. George Fyffe's 1863 notebook contains a sketch and suggested dimensions for a wharf, so he may have been involved in building it.
18. George Fyffe's Notebook, 11 December 1854.
19. William Ludstone Smith, Tytler Station Journal 1865-66, 11 January 1866.
20. *Marlborough Express*, 1 August 1862.
21. George Fyffe Papers, letter from Joseph Ward, 9 September 1863.
22. *Marlborough Press*, 24 February 1864.
23. *Marlborough Press*, 6 September 1865.
24. Register of Lands Sold, p. 42.
25. Sherrard, p.171.
26. Ibid. pp. 120-21; George Fyffe Papers, letter to Kitty, Nelson, 6 September 1865.
27. George Fyffe Papers, letter from J. Caverhill, 16 June 1867.
28. *Evening Post*, 21 November 1867.

NOTES TO CHAPTER FIVE

1. The spelling *Fyfe* was used in her diary.
2. *New Zealand Spectator & Cook Strait Guardian*, 20 October 1859.
3. Joseph Ward Diary, 26 January 1860; George Fyffe Papers: Joseph Ward letter to George Fyffe, 9 April 1860.
4. George Fyffe's Notebook, 6 January 1855, 6 April 1855.
5. George Fyffe's Notebook, 3 June 1854.
6. According to a drawing by the Rev. Codrington, dated January 1863.
7. Sketch dated 1867 from Kai Kōura Museum; Codrington sketch.
8. Trotter and McCulloch, *Fyffe's Revisited*, pp. 79-84. Their theory is that this was the store near which the moa egg was found in 1857.
9. Joseph Ward's Magnetic Field Books 69, pp. 77-8 and 70, p. 17.
10. Ibid; Codrington sketch.
11. Cochran, *Conservation Plan*, pp. 10, 13; Stephen Cashmore, *Fyffe House, Kaikoura. An Investigation and Report on Interior Decorative Finishes*. Report for the New Zealand Historic Places Trust, pp. 3-4.
12. George Fyffe's Notebook, 1854-55.
13. Sherrard, p. 286.
14. Ibid. p. 284.

15. Correspondence to Catherine Fyffe 1860-67, letter from Rev. Croasdaile Bowen, Riccarton, 1 August 1860.
16. Sherrard, pp. 285-6.
17. Ibid. p. 261.
18. W. L. Smith, Tytler Station Journal 1865-66, 12 December 1865.
19. Sherrard, pp. 262-3.
20. *Marlborough Press,* 4 April 1866; 21 November 1866; Sherrard, p. 263.
21. Sherrard, p. 162.
22. A Dr Fletcher seems to have been the first doctor — see, for example, *Kaikoura Herald and East Coast Advertiser,* 9 July 1870.
23. George Fyffe's Notebook 1863-64.
24. Joseph Ward's Magnetic Field Book 69, p. 77.
25. *Kaikoura Herald and East Coast Advertiser,* 21 August 1869.
26. *Kaikoura Herald and East Coast Advertiser,* 14 October 1871.

NOTES TO CHAPTER SIX

1. Richard S. Hill, *Policing the Colonial Frontier,* pp. 754, 765, 769.
2. Ibid. p. 765; *Marlborough Press,* 1 July 1865.
3. *Marlborough Press,* 1 June 1864; *Kaikoura Herald and East Coast Advertiser,* 18 September 1869.
4. *Marlborough Press,* 9 May 1866.
5. Ibid. 26 August 1865.
6. *Kaikoura Herald and East Coast Advertiser,* 24 February 1872.
7. Sherrard, p. 71.
8. Joseph Ward, Magnetic Field Book 69, p. 78.
9. Sherrard, p. 71.
10. *Marlborough Press,* 12 September 1863.
11. *Kaikoura Herald and East Coast Advertiser,* 30 July 1869.
12. Ibid. 22 July 1871.
13. Sherrard, pp. 177-9.
14. *Kaikoura Herald and East Coast Advertiser,* 18 September 1869, 18 December 1869.
15. Ibid. 10 July 1969, 17 July 1869.
16. Sherrard, p. 232.
17. *Kaikoura Herald and East Coast Advertiser,* 7 October 1868.
18. Ibid. 6 May 1871.
19. Ibid. 27 May 1871.
20. Ibid. 25 September 1869.
21. Ibid. 8 January 1870.
22. Sherrard, p. 233.
23. John O'C. Ross, *Pride in Their Ports,* p. 147.
24. Marine Department 4/4/2, letter of protest from local fishermen 4 August 1909; signatures include A. D. Goodall and J. Low.
25. Reminiscences of Mrs Rita Hansen, Kai Kõura.
26. S. O. 552, Field Book 182, p. 11.
27. Reminiscences of Mrs Rita Hansen, Kai Kõura.
28. DP 826, Plan of subdivision, Sections 224 and 400.

NOTES TO CHAPTER SEVEN

1. Search copy of Certificate of Title.
2. Sherrard, pp. 72-4.
3. *Marlborough Express,* 19 May 1920. Both launches were named after earlier whaleboats. The *Swiftsure* was 32 feet long with a speed of 17 miles an hour; the *Kersage* was 30 feet long with a speed of 23 to 25 miles per hour.
4. Sherrard, p. 90.
5. Search copy of Certificate of Title.
6. Ibid.
7. Sherrard, p. 235. The executors of Joseph Goodall's estate offered the site for lease in 1915, apparently without success. Marine Department 4/4/2, letter from Edward Goodall, 6 April 1915.
8. Interview with Charles Low, 24 July 1992.
9. Ibid.
10. Interviews with Charles Low, 24 July 1992 and Mary Reardon, 2 October 1992.
11. Stephen Cashmore, 'Peeling Back the Years', in *New Zealand Historic Places,* No. 38, September 1992, p. 9.

NOTES TO CHAPTER EIGHT

1. Interview with Charles Low, 24 July 1992.
2. Chris Cochran, *Fyffe House, Kaikoura: Conservation Plan,* p. 22.
3. Stephen Cashmore, *Fyffe House, Kaikoura. An Investigation and Report on Interior Decorative Finishes,* Report for the New Zealand Historic Places Trust, p. 3.

Family Trees

Fyffe Family Tree

Ann Scott (1743-1806) m. John Fyffe (1745-1810)

1. George (1787-1867) farmer, Stonehaven, Kincardine m. Christina ? sons, daughter as well as
   George (1827-1867) m. March 1860 **Catherine** Douglas Fyfe (d.1868)
   Margaret m. 1859 John McLean
      George Fyffe b. April 1860
2. Jean (d.1859) m. Daniel Reid (d.1830)
   William (d.1879) m. Isabella
      Annie m. ? Smith
3. James m. 1808 Elizabeth, dau. of Ellen Small and Alexander Stewart
   Helen (1809 -1834) m. William Bannerman (d.1836)
      Agnes m. Robert Davidson
      Margaret
      George
      Peter
   Alexander **Robert** b. Balgrie Mill and baptised Parish of St Martin's, Perthshire, 27 February 1811
   James and twin
   Elizabeth b. 1814; m. 1840 Thomas Laird (d.1851)
      William (1841-1928) — 6 children
      David (1843-1907)
      Mary Robina (1846-1916) m. Robert McKay — 6 children
      Robina (1849-1857)
4. William

From a family tree drawn up by Jennifer George, descendant of Elizabeth Laird.

Low Family Tree

Joseph Low, labourer m. Mary Dewar

Joseph Low born Arbroath, Scotland, 9.10.1856, died 7.5.1928. Fisherman and labourer.

m. c.1890 Maud Flint b. c.1874, d. 3.3.1950. Sister Annie, brother Fred, possibly others

1. Joseph d. 1891?
2. Frederick William (Fred) b. 1897, d. 1945 of cancer of the neck
3. Sidney Alexander b. c.1900, d. 16.11.74,
   m. 15.1.25 Doris May Harbott
   Gwendoline Violet Gray
   Josephine Rose Rickson
   Gordon Sidney
4. Mary Elizabeth (Bessie) b. c.1902, d. 20 or 22.2.72,
   m. Arthur Willis Oldman; 2 children died in infancy
5. Henry Joseph (Harry) b. c.1904, d. 16.11.57,
   m. Violet Harbott 1926-7 (sister of above)
   Charles b. 14.6.1928
   Alan
   Colin
   Irene
6. Douglas Donald b. c.1906, drowned 23.4.49,
   m. Sophia Reardon
   Kathleen, Douglas, Helen, Victor, Maree, Jenny
7. Frances Clara (Fanny) b. c.1908, d 2.8.79,
   m. Herbert Leslie Stove
   Maurice b. 1928, m. Shirley, dau. Michelle
8. Edward Charles (Ned) b. c.1910, d. 27.1.83,
   m. 3.11.43 Marjorie Oldman; four or five children
9. George b. c. 1912, d. 6.11.80

Joseph Low had seven other siblings; three others survived including Margaret, m. ? Soutar, cabinetmaker; their son Joseph Scott Soutar b. Arbroath c.1871, served with the U.S. Army in the Spanish-American War of 1898 and then in the Philippines. Arrived New Zealand 1921, described as seaman and fisherman, d. Kai Kōura 1.4.43.

From information provided by Gwen Gray, Josephine Rickson and Charles Low.

Bibliography

PRIMARY MATERIAL

Alexander Turnbull Library, Wellington

Hawkins, W., Sketchbook and Diary.
Plan of Town of Kaikoura, N16, c. 1873.
Plan of Town of Kaikoura, c. 1902.
Plan of Mt Fyffe Survey District, 834.2bje, 1879.
Plan showing Sections Nos. 29 to 37 and 40 to 48 inclusive on the Kincaid Run and Section No. 38 Kaikoura Suburban, purchased by G. Fyffe, Esq., May 16th 1865.
Wade, John, Letters 1842-46.
Ward, Joseph, Diaries 1860-62.

Canterbury Museum

Clifford, Charles, Papers.
Robert and George Fyffe Papers.
- Catherine Douglas Fyfe Diary 1859.
- Correspondence to Catherine Fyffe 1860-67.
- Farm Diary 1864.
- George Fyffe letters.
- G. Fyffe Day and Cash Book 1857.
- G. Fyffe Notebook 1854-55.
- G. Fyffe Notebook 1863-64.

Smith, W. L., Tytler Station Journal 1865-66.
Torlesse, C. O., Diary 1858-66.

Department of Survey and Land Information, Blenheim

Crown Grant Books.
Field Books 69, 70, 182, 358.
Magnetic Plan 858, Joseph Ward 1863.
Plans: SO 2A of Suburban Sections 369 and 347, March 1880.
- SO 2802, Town of Kaikoura, November 1863.
- SO 552, Sections 106-119, 7 February 1899.
- SO 1666, Town of Kaikoura, 4 November 1900.
- DP 826, Subdivision of Sections 224 and 400, 18 October 1920.

Register of Lands Sold.

Department of Justice Land Registry Office, Blenheim

Search of Title, 62 Avoca Street, Kaikoura.

Kaikoura Historical Society, Kaikoura Museum

Sherrard, J. M., notes.
Photograph collection.

National Archives, Wellington

Inward Correspondence of the Colonial Secretary, New Munster.
Marine Department File 4/4/2
Plan of the whaling station, LS-WG2 No. 530.
Robert Fyffe Estate Papers, No. 66.

Discussions with John Daniels, Director, New Zealand Historic Places Trust 1971-1987.

INTERVIEWS

Mary Forbes, interviewed by Cynthia Beavis, 2.10.92
Gwen Gray, interviewed by Cynthia Beavis, 3.7.92
Rita Hanson, interviewed by Denise Harris
Charles Low, interviewed by Cynthia Beavis, 24.7.92
Terence O'Donnell, interviewed by Cynthia Beavis, July 1992

NEWSPAPERS

Kaikoura Herald and East Coast Advertiser 1869-71 (Canterbury Public Library).
Evening Post, 21 November 1867 (Wellington Public Library).
Lyttelton Times, 5 August 1857 (Alexander Turnbull Library).
Marlborough Express (Alexander Turnbull Library).
Marlborough News and General Advertiser (Alexander

Turnbull Library).
Marlborough Press (Alexander Turnbull Library).

SECONDARY SOURCES

Published

Cashmore, Stephen, 'Peeling Back the Years', in *New Zealand Historic Places*, No. 38, September 1992, pp. 8-11.

Cochran, Chris, 'Conserving Fyffe House', in *New Zealand Historic Places,* No. 38, September 1992, pp. 4-7.

Day, Kelvin (comp.), *Shore Whaling,* Porirua Museum History Series, No. 1, Porirua Museum, Porirua, 1986.

Evison, Harry C., 'Kaikoura Whakatau' in Orange, Claudia (ed.), *Dictionary of New Zealand Biography*, Vol. 2, Bridget Williams Books/Department of Internal Affairs, Wellington, 1993.

Geelen, Anne, 'Historic Pa, Modern Marae', in *New Zealand Historic Places,* No. 38, September 1992, pp. 12-13.

Grady, Don, 'Fyffe, Alexander Robert' in Oliver, W. H. (ed.), *Dictionary of New Zealand Biography*, Vol. 1, Allen & Unwin/Department of Internal Affairs, Wellington, 1990.

Grady, Don, *Sealers and Whalers in New Zealand Waters,* Reed Methuen, Auckland, 1986.

Hill, Richard S., *The History of Policing in New Zealand, Volume One. Policing the Colonial Frontier: The Theory and Practice of Coercive Social and Racial Control in New Zealand, 1767-1867, Part Two,* GP Books/Department of Internal Affairs, Wellington, 1986.

McFadgen, B. G., 'Beach ridges, breakers and bones: late Holocene geology and archaeology of the Fyffe site, S49/46, Kaikoura Peninsula, New Zealand' in *Journal of the Royal Society of New Zealand,* Vol. 17, No. 4., 1987, pp. 381-394.

Morton, Harry, *The Whale's Wake,* John McIndoe Ltd, Dunedin, 1982.

Murphy, P. T., *BNZ Kaikoura, A Century of Service 1876-1976,* BNZ Archives, Wellington, 1976.

New Zealand Geographic Board, *He Kōrero Purakau mo Ngā Taunahanahatanga a Ngā Tūpuna/Place Names of the Ancestors, A Māori History Atlas,* New Zealand Geographic Board, Wellington, 1990.

Oliver, Stephen, 'Te Rauparaha' in Oliver, W. H. (ed.) *Dictionary of New Zealand Biography*, Vol. 1, Allen & Unwin/Department of Internal Affairs, Wellington, 1990.

Olssen, Erik, 'Where to from Here?', in *New Zealand Journal of History*, April 1992, pp. 55-7.

Ross, John O'C., *Pride in Their Ports,* Dunmore Press, Palmerston North, 1977.

Sherrard, J. M., *Kaikoura. A History of the District,* Kaikoura County Council, Christchurch, 1966.

Tau, Te Maire, Goodall, Anake, Palmer, David and Tau, Rakiihia, *Te Whakatau Kaupapa/Ngai Tahu Resource Management Strategy for the Canterbury Region,* Aoraki Press, Wgtn, November 1990.

Trotter, Michael M., 'Archaeological Investigations At Avoca Point, Kaikoura' in *Records of the Canterbury Museum,* Vol. 9, No. 4, June 1980, pp. 277-88.

Trotter, Michael M. and McCulloch, Beverley, *Fyffe's Revisited. Records of the Canterbury Museum,* Vol. 10, No. 7, May 1993, pp. 73-94.

Trotter, Michael M. and McCulloch, Beverley, *Unearthing New Zealand,* GP Books, Wellington, 1989.

Trotter, Michael M. and McCulloch, Beverley, *The Waiopuka Woolshed. Records of the Canterbury Museum.* Vol. 10, No. 9, May 1993, pp 107-116.

Unpublished

Cashmore, Stephen, 'Fyffe House, Kaikoura. An Investigation and Report on Interior Decorative Finishes' Report for the New Zealand Historic Places Trust, Wellington, May 1991.

Cashmore and Colleagues, 'A Report on the Relationship Between the Original Decorative Scheme at Fyffe House, Kaikoura, and Established Victorian Principles of Colour and Decoration', Auckland, August 1992.

Cochran, Chris, 'Fyffe House, Kaikoura. Conservation Plan 1990'. Report for the New Zealand Historic Places Trust, Wellington, 1990, and Addendum.

Dictionary of New Zealand Biography data file on Alexander Robert Fyffe

George, J., Fyffe family tree, 1979.

Harris, Jan, 'Fyffe House', report for the New Zealand Historic Places Trust, Wellington, 1988

New Zealand Historic Places Trust files: reports and correspondence.

Trotter, Michael M. and McCulloch, Beverley, 'The Fyffe Historic Precinct Kaikoura', Christchurch, January 1991.

Index

A Wellingtonian, Jan Harris graduated from Victoria University in 1984 and is a historian with the New Zealand Historic Places Trust head office. She has written *Alberton and its Family* and *A Handbook for Researchers,* both published by the Trust in 1990, and several articles for the Trust's magazine *New Zealand Historic Places*. She has just completed a postgraduate Diploma in Museum Studies through Massey University. She has two adult sons and two grandchildren.